Freedom in Religion or Freedom from Religion

The Great American Cultural War between Traditionalists and Secularists

James Larry Hood

Hamilton Books
A member of
The Rowman & Littlefield Publishing Group
Lanham • Boulder • New York • Toronto • Plymouth, UK

Copyright © 2010 by
Hamilton Books
4501 Forbes Boulevard
Suite 200
Lanham, Maryland 20706
Hamilton Books Acquisitions Department (301) 459-3366

Estover Road
Plymouth PL6 7PY
United Kingdom

Library of Congress Control Number: 2009943732
ISBN: 978-0-7618-5049-6 (paperback : alk. paper)
eISBN: 978-0-7618-5050-2

Contents

Introduction

Beginning in the 1960s, the post-World War II American baby boom generation went to war with itself over what social/political values should or would
hold them and future generations together as a civilization and as a nation.
On one side, Traditionalists held to what had been a common understanding
of the nature of family, the functions of government, and the role of religion
in one's personal and public life. On the other side, Secularists rejected all
the old understandings and pushed hard for a new and, to them, far better
world order. The desperate dispute focused on the fundamental question of
who Americans are as a people and looked even beyond that to confront the
thought that now no such people really exist nor should they. To date there
has been no cessation of hostilities.

Each side insists that it is the true champion of freedom and that the other
is a destroyer of individual liberty. The cultural war is the latest eruption of
a two millennial old clash in the West between reason and faith and a manifestation of the primordial, ever-ongoing struggle between order and chaos.
As both sides well understand, the stakes are high. In this book two essays
consider first what can be thought of as traditional American values and second, what are the very different values that give Secularists their vision of a
new order.

As the titles of the two essays indicate, religion lies at the core of the
American dispute, for all definitions of community (or nation) are first and
last assumptions concerning ultimate values and the nature of the cosmos
(or man) that must be held in common for a community to exist. For Traditionalists the Judeo-Christian faith as filtered through Western history
and the particular American experience is the well-spring of freedom. For
Secularists such religion (distorted or not) is all too often the great enemy

of individualism and personal and communal liberty. Consequently little border land or middle ground in America's Great Cultural War exists. Consequently, also, for those knowingly and willingly in the war, its proper resolution is of ultimate importance.

Freedom in Religion: Contemporary American Traditionalists' Understanding of National Culture and Government

Founded on the expansive and deep dreams of dissenting English Protestant-ism and of the western Enlightenment, the United States understandably has never been a homogeneous nation of people of like attitudes and minds cher-ishing all the same cultural values. One-third of American colonials refused to rebel against England and left for other parts of the Empire. After that, there have been three long-term eras of great divide among Americans. Until the end of their Civil War, citizens of the United States repeatedly clashed over the existence of slavery in the southern states. For decades before and then after the Civil War, the nation was one of great and increasing unrest over the amalgamation of many millions of Catholic immigrants (who began arriving in the 1830s and 1840s) with a Protestant people, an at-times-seething unrest that did not subside until the election of John Kennedy nearly a hundred years after the Civil War. Since then there has been and remains a growing cultural chasm between the traditional religious conservatives and the modern, liberal secularists. There can be no accurate encompassing view of the chasm with-out an understanding of who the conservatives are and what they believe, what present day American liberals position themselves against.[1]

Actually the present divide had its beginnings long ago, well over a century ago, as large numbers of people, hemmed in by the constricted, limited capi-talism of rural lands (i.e. more people than land), moved off America's farms to its cities and were joined there by Catholic immigrants, from rural lands themselves. The United States had become more than half urban by 1920, and the continuing mass exodus of men and women off the farms after World War II kept increasing the population and power of an urban environment far different from that of small towns and farms where it did often seem that everyone knew everyone else's business. The urban environment, in contrast,

1

had over time allowed people more easily to slip out of the restraints of family and community into anonymity in the crowd.

The old order was fading. It did not matter anymore in the new broader scheme of things what people's family names were or what church they went to or their politics or their reputation for honesty and hard work. These had mattered greatly when community life meant life in the town and country. But by World War I the town was giving way to the city, the county to the state, and the state to Washington, D.C., a process much accelerated during the Great Depression. Now it mattered what large state and national interest groups people were part of, such as the Farm Bureau, the Union, the Medical Association, National Retailers, etc. Locally, whether in the small town or the ethnic neighborhood, the family and church might matter, but not belonging to such large scale, wide-reaching money interest groups meant being ineffectual in state and national affairs that now impinged far more upon people's lives than ever before.

Nevertheless, such large-scale interest groups could not provide or create community. Consequently, there still was no national culture of common values and like-thinking people as the nation divided after World War I along regional, religious, racial, and ethnic lines. All these lines cut into one another: with Protestants divided north and south and theologically, Catholics by ethnicity, and rural Protestants opposing urban Catholics. Protestants defined the world in terms of abstract law and principles, justice and independent action. Catholic immigrants (not so much English Catholics who had been colonials) lived in a corporate world of hierarchy, deference, personal obligation, and loyalty.[2]

In the early twentieth century, American progressive intellectuals and academics actually consciously worked and wrote for a strong, cosmopolitan nationalism, but they wanted a national unity devoid of federalism and localism, "a conception of citizenship that. . . . Entailed the duty of reflecting on and articulating ideas of national public good *unmediated* [emphasis added] by party, interest, region, or sectarian religion." Such people "saw the university as something like a national 'church'—the main repository and protector of common values, common American meanings, and common American identities." These men and women lost out politically, then, to those who did not want to surrender their particular faiths to a national church of the university. But they and their learned successors on campuses continued to preach and write in a similar vein throughout the twentieth century, eventually reaching many Americans more willing to consider seeking a national, pragmatic General Will devoid of intermediaries.[3]

In the meantime people found no common religion, no common set of ultimate, political values, and no common definition, at times, of the meaning of life itself. Until more purely religious values could be merged into ultimate political values that served as a common secular religion that reached across and supported localities, ethnic/racial communities, states, regions, and differing religious faiths, little sense of an overarching national community could exist. By necessity, then, the New Deal of the 1930s, the governmental programs of the Democratic Party, was the product of an alliance of people who did not understand or like each other. Urban, northern Catholics; rural, southern white, evangelical (often fundamentalist) Protestants; and formerly southern African Americans now in their own northern enclaves did not speak at all about shared faith or religious vision that could reinforce everyone's sense of commonality: they could not together address moral/value issues and concentrated instead on practical, money issues and jobs, both controlled by local party people. Teddy Roosevelt's supporters in 1912 after they nominated him for President had sung "Onward Christian Soldiers." Twenty years later, at the birth of the New Deal, Franklin Roosevelt's followers at his nomination sang "Happy Days are Here Again."[4]

Shared adversity, however, did help to bring people together. All had to endure the Great Depression. All had to fight in World War II and Korea. Racial minorities achieved greater integration of public institutions like the military and schools. All had to endure the Cold War. As time passed, Catholic immigrants, who had full equal political rights and freedom and opportunity to prosper, served their country in the military and in all levels of government and adopted as their own the old national political myths about a promised land and the Declaration's proclamation of the God-given, universal rights of all people. Irish Catholic John F. Kennedy in 1960 proclaimed himself a citizen of the old Puritan City on a Hill and won the Presidency.

In the 1960s just as Protestants and Catholics had come together on common ground, America went to war with itself on a new front. The racial and ethnic divides were still there, as well as a growing gender divide. All merged into a great religious-secular chasm as a new political/social left sought benefits and rights for new interest groups not grounded, the Secularists insisted, in religion-infused morality but rather based on identities intentionally distinctive from, even superseding, a common national identity intertwined with western religion.

At very nearly the same time religious fundamentalists, now blended with evangelicals, reemerged in the 1970s and 1980s with great power and with great anger over what appeared to them as an extraordinary and dangerous decline in the personal and social morality necessary for community cohesiveness. They were joined in this sentiment by a sizable portion of the now Americanized Catholic community, which found itself identifying with the social/moral concerns of conservative Protestants: "This evolution on the right reflected a crucial double shift in American history: the decline of anti-Catholicism among white Protestants and the rise of a politically and theologically conservative Catholicism that put sexual morality, traditional gender roles, biblical truths, and the protection of Christianity above church teachings on labor [and capitalism] the death penalty, and social welfare." And both social conservative groups were reinforced by political conservatives that feared a dangerous circumscribing of individual liberty by a mass democracy polity without intermediate social groupings that blended loyalties to as well as pride in local communities with love of nation. As Allan J. Lichtman noted: "In an ironic but not surprising twist of history, white evangelical Protestants gave Catholic conservative candidate Patrick J. Buchanan his most enthusiastic support in the Republican presidential primaries of 1996 and the most devout Catholics preferred evangelical Protestant George W. Bush to Catholic John Kerry in the presidential election of 2004."[5]

Traditionalists saw little social cohesion and respect for values left. Marriage rates and birth rates had declined. The number of divorces had risen substantially. Sexual relations outside marriage were natural and liberating. Children with no fathers were everywhere. Gays insisted that same sex marriages (with children) were at least the equivalent to heterosexual marriages. Fatherhood was an anachronism. Youth confessed to cheating and stealing on a grand scale and did not feel guilty about it. In fact guilt, itself, was a bad thing, anti-liberating. Bibles and prayers had been taken out of public schools, and prophylactics had been brought in. Christmas had been reduced to a winter solstice festival. Some had insisted and insisted still that "In God We Trust" be removed from all public structures and property. People were demanding rights and privileges and advancements based not on their personhood or their ability or their achievement but on identification with interest groups, tribes really—the very opposite of a national people. Instead of Americans striving to be one people out of many, now Americans sought to be many different people out of one. American values and ways were compared to those of other peoples and nations and always found by Secularists, it seemed, greatly lacking, even though the idea of moral absolutes had been rejected. And even American government (especially the nonelected parts such as courts and bureaucrats) seemed often to be supportive of all this. Those three pillars of American civilization, those of family, religion, and government by the people, were crumbling, hammered to bits by a new generation of Americans wanting a vastly different American civilization, a multicultural nation and a multicultural, transnational world.[6]

This long-term divide was quite evident in the 2008 presidential election. In the midst of a long, unpopular war and a desperate credit crisis, the more conservative candidate (in terms addressed here), though of the party of the unpopular, incumbent President received forty-six percent of the popular vote, losing by six percent. The voters divided along a line that had arrayed on one side more of the older, more of the non-urban, more of the married, more of the religious (especially evangelical Protestants), more of the less educated, fewer union members, more of the charitable, more white Americans (especially males). On the other side, were more of the younger, far more of the urban, more of the unmarried (sixty-three percent of unmarried women), more of the secular, more of the well-educated, more union members, fewer of the charitable, more nonwhite Americans. The line split the Catholic vote, with those attending church regularly on one side, the less observant on the other. A look particularly at education, marriage, and religious data of the 2008 presidential election strongly indicates a continuing division in the country between traditional religious people and modern secularists, or more pointedly, using theological terms, between those of a God-centered world and those of a man-centered world.[7]

Indeed, religion is the single most important factor in both defining and dividing Americans. This has always been so. The Great Awakening in the colonies in the 1730s and 1740s (which divided the religious at the time) democratized politics and gave people a much greater sense of their individual worth regardless of their station in society. "What do we mean," wrote John Adams, "by the American Revolution; it was only an effect and consequence of it. The Revolution was in the minds of the people . . . a change in their religious sentiments." Furthermore, Washington, Adams, Jefferson, and men like them at the founding of the nation, though deeply influenced by the Enlightenment and not necessarily orthodox or dogmatic Christians themselves, assumed and were very insistent that there could be no American republic without Christianity. The Great Revival of the early nineteenth century stoked the fires of democratic expansion and political reform to still greater heights. Evangelical Protestantism gave the nation its cultural unity. Early twentieth century Democratic and Republican Progressivism (a two decades long drive for social and political reform) was a secular manifestation of American Protestantism. In the nineteenth and twentieth centuries Protestants and Catholics remained divided (with the Vatican strongly anti-republican much of that time) until, as already noted, the election of John Kennedy and the Church's internal reformation with Vatican II, Pope John XXIII's *Pacem in Terris* (1963), and Jesuit Father John Courtney Murray's assertion that "religious freedom is rooted in the very dignity of the human person." Today's Secularists resist (in the name of freedom) any reference to a common heritage springing from religious belief, such references being a diminution of the liberty of those of many differing faiths not part of the western tradition. President Obama in his 2009 inaugural address made pointed reference to the contributions to American society made by people of many divergent faiths and pointedly made no reference at all to any foundational faith from which came the ideals of freedom, individual worth, and self-government.[8]

What does religion mean to American conservatism today? That there is order and meaning to the world, human life and individuals have intrinsic worth and rights and obligations, that there are moral absolutes, there is justice and mercy, that time has purpose (a beginning and an end), that life is filled with wonder, adventure, calling, and surprise, that three things abide—faith, hope, love—, that the Bible provides an unparalleled description of human nature, that the greatest goal or good is not self-realization but self denial and sacrifice, and that there is a God without Whom none of the other above listed elements of reality exist. Though they might not know of him they would agree with one of Europe's greatest atheists, Nietzsche, who recognized that the West was built upon a foundation of ideas and ideals all of which came from and are dependent on Christianity, no matter how secular they may appear today, and that western civilization (including its reverence for individual freedom) cannot retain its hallmark ideals without the faith that gave those ideals life.[9]

Traditionalists in the United States (whether or not they are orthodox and church going or more like Jefferson) understand religion as the source and sustainer of freedom, unlike Europe where freedom has often been defined in opposition to religion. Traditionalists, because of American colonial and national history, again in contrast to European history, believe pluralism in religion and subcultures and states (federalism), all subsumed by one national culture of liberty and republicanism (understood as secularized Christian dogma) a very good thing. American Traditionalists tend to believe in their nation as a City on a Hill, whether as an example or an active agent in world affairs. They understand Lincoln's words about the nation as "man's last best hope," and they can see a parallel between the Old Testament's chosen people as a blessing to the earth and America's exceptionalism being a means to uphold and promote to the world universal values. The Statue of Liberty still has meaning, as do the Jefferson and Lincoln memorials in the nation's capital.[10]

Judeo-Christian tenets define for American Traditionalists, both the devout and the less so, their understanding of human nature which in turn serves as the basis of their understanding of the purposes and parameters of community and government. Man is a created being endowed by his Creator with inalienable rights to life and liberty (and free will). Happiness is a right appearing perhaps in apocrypha. God has set eternity in his heart. As such he is a tragic figure, never quite at home, never fully at rest, never whole. Though made a little less than the angels, he is never-the-less prone to evil, to the self-will without which he cannot survive outside Eden. On his own he cannot return to the Garden but must travel on to take up his destiny as ruler and caretaker of the earth, a role in which he finds work to be both a blessing and a curse. Actually he cannot go on alone but must have a woman. Family is the primordial institution. Only grace can take him home. In the meantime he can build and acquire, create and destroy, love and be loved or hate and be hated. All life requires suffering and sacrifice. All these elements of human nature can be found in the Garden of Eden story. In keeping with his dual nature man can work for and earn happiness, if fortunate, and, if blessed, he will experience that which he cannot earn—now and then, here and there he will be surprised by joy.[11]

For all Traditionalists the key understanding is that of tragedy, the necessity of striving, soaring on hope above flaws. For the religious Traditionalists, it is also "remember thy Creator" and redemption. Increasingly so, the ideas of creation and tragedy are yet another cause of division between American Traditionalists and present day Secularists.

In *Antigone*, the great tragedian Sophocles of ancient Greece two and a half millennia ago examined the inescapable moral dilemmas that arise as individuals seek to live up to a personal code while being a part of a group of people, a community with societal standards not always identical to those of the individual. God placed a mark on Cain so others would leave him alone after his murder of his brother and so he could live among other human beings. In the context of the story, Cain's question to God "Am I my brother's keeper?" carries with it the answer: yes. Community is a necessary part of human existence if there is to be anything called civilization; in the West community and the individual are always in paradoxical tension.

All civilizations are based on paradoxes, on tensions between opposite values. In the West the great tension has been that between the rights/freedom of the individual and rights/authority of the community. Michael Kammen asserts that compared to even the rest of the West, even more so for the rest of the world, the paradoxes that allow a particular American civilization are extraordinarily tense, taut, and ever in-play and that probably most Americans have some intuitive sense of this condition and are not only comfortable with it but prefer it. They like keeping liberty and equality in tension.[12]

Until after World War II and especially after 1960, when the post World War I fissures of the present cultural divide greatly expanded, nearly all had a common understanding of local or home community, whether they grew up in a Southern Baptist town or Little Italy or Chicago's Southside; people knew neighbors, went to church for worship services and socials, attended lodge and club meetings, took pride in local youth's academic and athletic accomplishments and had family reunions, complete with both patriarchs and matriarchs. Such communities gave people multiple identities.

Pluralism, outside the local community, but within a Judeo-Christian culture and political principles derived from dissenting English Protestantism, was prized because it allowed every locality to hold to its own particularities, at least to a considerable degree, and paradoxically it allowed people to reach out to people in other parts of the nation in two very different ways. Members of a particular denomination in a town shared a common faith with others of the denomination scattered across the nation. But citizens of towns with common folkways could also feel very secure in that local identity; they knew who they were, when communicating and working with others from different places and different folkways. This had always been true of Protestants interacting with other Protestants—Freemasons reached across localities and faiths—and was true also of Protestants and Catholics after mid-twentieth century, with some Catholics later still, with Vatican permission, joining Masonic organizations.[13]

Almost all Americans of every political/religious persuasion have always been people of progress (the secular version of God's Will or Providence), and for Americans there have always been modern times and change, and that in turn has involved a continual expansion of the boundaries of community. The first coastal settlements had western frontiers; as people moved west, there were the old settlements and the new. The Great Awakening and the Great Revival both were in part an effort to create community in the new West and to integrate it into the older Union.[14]

Bill Sunday's late nineteenth century revival sermons were yet another effort to recreate community, this time for those who had moved off the farms to the cities. Still over time even ethnic enclaves, Protestant and Catholic, lost power to hold and give identity to those there. In the last half of the twentieth century, modernization inevitably brought about a mass, urban culture where old ties and ways of identifying one's self faded away. Thus as early as 1950, David Riesman could write a book on American culture entitled *The Lonely Crowd* about the individual lost and alone while surrounded by people. Natan Sharensky in his *Defending Liberty* has warned that such loss of smaller group identities atomizes people and leaves them defenseless against big government, big business, big anything, even, or most importantly, big (or mass) democracy. The individual who has no identity outside the mass is rootless. American novelist and social critic, Wendell Berry, has been insistent that one of the great weaknesses of present day American society is the autonomous individual, especially those who adjust to being libertines, for such people represent the eventual destruction (ironically) of individuals, families, and communities that protect people and their rights from great aggregates of power. Co joined with and integrated with being believers, this understanding of community and rootedness most distinguishes today's true Traditionalists from today's Secularists.[15]

This modern rootlessness underlies calls after the 2008 presidential election, like after other presidential elections, for the abolishment of the Electoral College and its replacement with one mass, national vote. But one of the things that federalism does is create balances of power by creating multiple identities and like interests, including loyalties and associations with states, where government meets everyday life. The College helps keep this federalism alive. Traditionalists would not be supportive of such proposals.

Traditionalists are fearful of both mass politics and the extreme individualism (with its abdication of citizenship's studied responsibilities) that it promotes. The individual in the city or in the great corporation finds that as such he has considerable freedom from the old social standards and restraints of neighbors, churches and social groups and thus finds comfortable and desirable a mass democratic politics that leaves him alone, except again for mass participation via rallies and the Internet. Intermediate organizations are unnecessary to such an individual and undesirable because they can impose social/ethical restraints and make too many personal demands. This leads not only to profound rootlessness but also very importantly a longing (always unrecognized by those experiencing such) for a messiah and a great temptation and tendency towards seeking meaning in mass populist movements that, without intermediaries between the individual and the masses, can lead to action absent reflection and contemplation without knowledge. All such things are overwhelmed by the need to belong, to be on a mission that provides meaning and worth. Traditionalists understand such conditions lead to loss of liberty.

Compounding this problem has been the intentional abandonment before World War I of the idea of public education as character/citizen building and the intentional and insistent abandonment over the last forty years by higher education of liberal arts and western values (roots) that have been denigrated and denounced by American universities. Traditionalists see the old social groupings of schools, churches, clubs, lodges, and local political party organizations as necessary and far safer than mass movements/organizations as everyday-living-and-human-association sources and builders of leaders, leaders imbued with values that can create inspired and inspiring vision that both defines a people and directs them toward the future beyond a mass of existential individuals who seek above all else to be unrestrained personally and unburdened by personal responsibility, at a one-on-one level.

Further, Traditionalists understand the necessity of vision that holds a people together. They heed the Old Testament warning: where there is no vision (revelation) the people cast off restraint (die). For Traditionalists vision is tied to wisdom and that to a right understanding of man's condition in a world of tragedy and grace where liberty and responsibilities are a paradox, where man must accept his limitations but dream of building new worlds, where he must strive to be just while offering mercy, where he is blessed with the spiritual gifts of faith, hope, and love to make the most of life and his creative power, where freedom also is a wondrous gift of God.[16]

Reiterating, Traditionalists (social or political, devout or not so much) understand the world as framed by the Old and New Testaments. For them religious belief is a necessity for a people to endure and prosper. One cannot, as Weigel says Europe has done, be indifferent to faith and consequently think of leaders expressing religious thought and imagery as fanatical and xenophobic. Lincoln, the man many consider America's greatest President and a man never belonging to any church, would be viewed as a mad man by such Europeans and by many of today's Secular Americans with his vision and words and prayers of sin, judgment, humbleness, forgiveness, and charity.[17]

In a terrible irony, mass democracy, having reduced the organizations and locales that could produce good leaders, has made American leaders squeamish when referencing the truths of faith, very resistant to doing so, leaving the people with indifference and no vision of their own. For Traditionalists it is a lamentable state when Americans all share a common knowledge of the wicked witch of the West and her winged monkeys but do not know what is meant by Moses on Mt. Sinai. Traditionalists understand that without a common vision leadership must decline. They understand that in the West, where the truth of man's right to freedom emerged, if one cannot reach back to the past to draw strength to press on into the future, one cannot purposefully press on. Man can only wander. If leaders cannot frame communicated thought in terms of once and future homes, they have no community of people to lead. Consequently, American Traditionalists and Secularists view each other across a great chasm with no bridge, for there can be no common vision that allows them together to build one.

Going further, for there to be rewarding human life and a united people there must also be a shared sense of adventure. Writing in *Let Us Have Faith*, Helen Keller said, "Life is either a daring adventure or nothing. To keep our faces toward change and behave like free spirits in the presence of fate is strength undefeatable." Quoting the 1960s television show Star Trek, humankind is "to boldly go where no man has gone before," or, according to Western scripture, to go out from Eden to subdue and have dominion over the earth: to multiply, to explore, discover, build, enjoy; to know and love one another (love being man's one true creative act); to understand the Golden Rule as a command to action in seeking one another's well-being; to build community. How one carries out such actions justly, how one lives the adventure, often divides Traditionalists and divides Traditionalists from Secularists in the United States, for example how or when to multiply or how does one best serve as a caretaker of the earth.[18]

In possession of a terrible liberty to do both good and evil, how does man best rule himself? The founding fathers' rejected Hobbes' understanding of human nature as nasty, brutish, and short, absent a higher, unchallengeable authority to order and command. They also rejected what Rousseau would call the General Will, a mystical, mass democracy authoritarianism. Instead they insisted that man could rule himself provided he put brakes or safeguards around his own acknowledged worse nature. Since power wielded by either the one or the many would be abused, governmental power had to have checks and balances, enough power to actually govern but not so much as to become despotic. As Madison would suggest in *Federalist* X all of society involved continually pitting one man's ambition against another, one interest group against another, one region against another, where no one and no group would have all power. Elections would become civil, peaceful, non-violent revolutions. As a further protection, the first Congress sent to the states for ratification constitutional amendments that would become known as the Bill of Rights against governmental encroachments of personal and individual state liberties.

The federal system established by the Constitution encouraged people to identify not only with the nation but with their states and their localities, with citizens operating in and directing many overlapping spheres that contend with one another, thus protecting liberty. Rousseau's General Will is thwarted by this federalism and a central government of three contending branches, with the legislative branch, itself, split into two houses that must agree for a bill to become law. Only the lower house is democratic if democracy is defined in terms of one-man-one-vote. Thus, deliberation and a due respect of minority positions are encouraged. American Traditionalists recognize that the argument for ending the Electoral College can be applied as well to the United States Senate and cannot see the abolition of the Senate in the name of mass democracy a good thing.[19]

The Constitution's system of checks and balances has failed once. For seventy-five years it staved off conflict and war over the twin disputes present at the birth of the nation: concerning the continuation of slavery and the very meaning of the federal union, itself. But eventually war came, as abolitionist William Lloyd Garrison (quoting Isaiah 28:15) phrased it, to put an end to the Constitution (because it allowed slavery) as a "covenant with death and an agreement with hell" and to better secure the federal union with all its deliberative democracy as "man's last best hope."

American Traditionalists understand their federal union to be an extremely valued safeguard of liberty, precisely because it provides unity in the ideal of self-government and in multiple identities for its citizens, a unity which prevents their isolation and atomization by the government and just as importantly reduces the opportunities of someone riding in on a white horse leading a left wishing to enforce the General Will or a right weary of republicanism. Along with a common language, overarching ideals keep the United States from becoming a Tower of Babel, or, referencing more modern times, the Balkan Peninsula or Iraq. Also, the political right, with its focus on such ideals, acts as a brake on the social/religious right, itself, transforming into a populist, mass movement looking for a political savior that will enforce righteousness (desired social standards). The social right returns the favor sometimes by contrasting the values of capitalism and the possibility of being all a person can be with those of service and sacrifice—a rare, but very important (even if a shaky and shifting) common ground the social right shares with the political left.[20]

The great modern irony is that the American left, with its social wing that seeks autonomy to the point of the libertine with no social responsibilities, actually reduces liberty. The political left, in seeking to find and carry out the General Will for all of life's problems (often with genuine compassion) has for a generation now used political and institutional power (academia, news media, large corporate employers, bureaucrats and courts) to enforce both politically correct thought and speech as a counter to social norms of the right. The American right sees the left as like much of the rest of the West (Europe and Canada) where one must not, upon pain of fine and imprisonment, speak ill of others or their religions. Another irony, almost always unrecognized, is that it is the American Traditionalists who best understand that unless people can disagree, even, and most especially, about religion, there is no liberty. They also understand that the American left no longer understands this or that they are severely circumscribing what they cherish most—individual expression.[21]

This ghastly irony illustrates how difficult it is in the West even now to have both individual liberty and community. Quite obviously, figuring out how to have both deeply divides American Traditionalists and Secularists. How do people boldly go while being their brother's keeper? How do they help their neighbor without diminishing him? How do they rule the earth without destroying it? How do they reconcile the freedom to be all they can be (the great goal of both the political right and the social left) with community responsibilities? How do they insist on common values without endangering liberty and how do they insist on no absolutes without dehydrating community?

Today's American Traditionalists, drawing upon a heritage and history and culture built on the values of dissenting English Protestants, base their answers to all these questions upon their understanding of American liberty being a product of western religious values (in God's eyes there is no Jew or Greek, male or female, slave or free) and their own country's particular culture and religious expressions. For American Traditionalists their individual freedom, even the separation of church and state, comes from religion and from the way religion has been proclaimed in the American community, including Jefferson's Declaration that all men are created equal, an understanding that sets them apart from much of the rest of the world, even much of the West that often defines liberty as freedom from religion.[22]

Politics then is a question of religion, the ultimate values and understanding of reality that one tries to live by. For Traditionalists the existential individual is not a defender of liberty, merely a practitioner dependent upon the efforts of others he ignores, and eventually the existentialist is a destroyer of liberty. Contrariwise, Traditionalists see themselves as defending and promoting liberty by defending and promoting social cohesion. Comparatively speaking, Traditional men and women do not live alone. They marry more often, have more children, and have less unwed pregnancies. They go to church more often, give away more for those in need, volunteer time more, and are more trusting of others around them. In all this the Traditionalists provide the necessary mediation between the individual and mass society.[23]

All this means that Americans, with Traditionalists and their opponents each seeking liberty and well-being, have divided and remain divided over the most basic and fundamental arch types of civilization, with both sides seeing the other as a destroyer of liberty and well-being. The primordial clash of order and chaos goes on as does that of the city versus the outlying areas. The Traditionalists insist on being rooted in a religious world view that accepts the tragic nature of man, himself. The American Traditionalist-Secularist clash is yet another manifestation of the two millennia old tension across the West between Jerusalem (God) and Athens (man).

Those of the farther left in America reject the Traditionalists' world view because they have no identity in it and it provides them with no sense of worth. Where and who is the person not married with children, not going to church and not attending club/lodge meetings? If that person is not in the broadest sense socially connected? If he or she is not part of the old guard WASPs with their traditionalist Catholic and Jewish allies? In the 2008 presidential election fifty-eight percent of unmarried men and sixty-three percent of unmarried women, with an increasing number remaining childless, voted for Obama; the three highest birth-rate states were red (Utah, Nebraska, and

Idaho) and the three lowest were blue (New Hampshire, Vermont, and incredibly Rhode Island).[24]

Fear and loathing between the more Traditional and the more Secular have reached such levels that in 2007 a national poll found thirty-five percent of Democratic party members believed that President Bush knew about the 9/11 attacks in advance and twenty-six were not sure. The left saw Bush as the ultimate WASP and Obama as the new and necessary Everyman and as such maybe even a savior. In one final irony, on Sunday before the inauguration at festivities at the Lincoln Memorial, Episcopal bishop, the Rev. V. Gene Robinson, who had been invited to give an invocation precisely because he was a partnered, gay priest, found it necessary to remind the half-million celebrators that the incoming President "is a human being, not a messiah."[25]

Traditionalists had trouble even hearing Obama because for them he appeared a rootless Nowhereman engendered by a progressive, pragmatic, devoutly secular academia. On the same Sunday as Robinson's prayer, one of the new President's oldest political allies, Chicago university professor William Ayers, having been invited by the University of Toronto to lecture there, was denied entry into Canada by Canadian immigration authorities because of his criminal history. Obama's association with Ayers, the old Weatherman founder/bomber, and with another preacher, his own long-time G-D-America pastor, caused no concern on the left, for such associates merely identified him as a typical citizen of the new, rising, multicultural, transnational American university world. Traditionalists had a different understanding.[26]

Freedom from Religion: America's Newest Left, the Secular Ideologues, and Their Vision of a New National Culture and Government

THE EVIL OF A NATIONAL IDENTITY

Freedom is a hallmark of American civilization. Still even the word "freedom" can mean extraordinarily different things to different people. In the present United States an amorphous group of citizens have identified freedom as the supreme value and in such a way as to challenge intentionally and directly the foundational values of the traditional (that is western and more specifically British in origins) culture of the nation, now deemed by such people as not the well-spring and sustainer of freedom but rather an oppressive civilization, the values of which are a threat to true individualism and self-realization.

Paradoxically, this latest manifestation of the American Left by and large has rejected traditional structures, such as family and religious congregations, institutions that have protected the individual by serving as bulwarks against anomie and atomization of the individual in the face of great governmental power. Instead, it has sought to use governmental fiat (mostly bureaucratic and judicial) to create a new identity for individuals within new, larger group identities based on gender/race/ethnicity, with the groups themselves claiming, as groups, prerogatives and benefits. It seeks the reverse of "out of many one"; it seeks "out of one many." The Secular Ideologues strongly oppose much of the western world's traditional ethos and the American nation's will to power (but no one else's, at times appearing to even rejoice in other's exercise of power). Since the western concept of tragedy is unknown to them or if known rejected, they never perceive or consider their own susceptibility to the will to power and the threat they themselves pose to the freedom they cherish. The paradoxes and internal contradictions of the Newest Left are so extreme that any semblance of a coherent ideology is impossible and that unity of thought and action is found only in identifying

15

a common enemy, identifying in Professor Richard Stennet's words "the evil of a national identity."[1]

This new Left has labeled the old culture, out of which arose the very concepts of freedom and individualism they cherish, evil and beyond redemption and seeks a new order, to begin the world anew, much like the founding fathers of the United States did. But the founding fathers were sustained by deep theological, philosophical, and scientific roots in western culture and were seeking to preserve, protect, and enhance a freedom they already knew, a degree of liberty unparalleled in history: to protect the ancient "rights of Englishmen." The left bank of the present American cultural divide contrariwise is by conscious choice a rootless, existential exercise—its closest ideological cousin being a communism which has dreamed of a someday naturally virtuous people (with a single identity as human beings) and a stateless society, but which has appealed to group identities suppressed by greater powers either national or imperial in order to overcome and dispel those greater powers.

This newest Left is driven by a passion for freedom that has become an ideology of unrestrained individualism, unformed and uninformed by well-thought out ideas or themes. In 2008, the finale of the television series "Boston Legal" has two straight men fighting for and winning in Massachusetts state court the right to marry while telling gay opponents (who feared such action would only provide more arguments for opponents of gay marriage) that it was none of their business what they did in their personal lives. The Secular Left proudly confesses it is at war on behalf of self-expression with those it sees standing on the right bank of the cultural divide.[2]

In this newest order, coherence of thought or ideals is irrelevant. Consequently the paradoxes of life are magnified and intensified. Only the individual free of the old order is relevant. The individual seeks greater freedom through, not national identity, but group identities that are grounded on what one is by birth (gender/race/ethnicity), not by what one does or thinks. Yet, the possibility of biological imperatives or determinants is denied. Everything is a social construct that can be undone and rebuilt, especially considering heterosexual relationships. Then again just the opposite is assumed if considering homosexual imperatives: universities should offer domestic partner benefits to employees so the schools can attract gay professors who, because they are gay, are more creative.[3]

The Secular Ideologues have an ethereal vision of what could and should be in a new civilization and have attempted to draw on thoughts and attitudes from the old, traditional culture that, because of life-long familiarity (but not any real relationship to the new vision), could serve at least for a while as foundational pillars for their better world. But to do so the Secular Left has uprooted the old ideals and values from their historical development and meaning and twisted those values into new meanings that lack substance, coherence and consistency and their new form cannot truly sustain this newest vision of self-fulfilled individuals.

THE OLD CONSTRUCT

As described by Samuel Huntington, the old construct that Secularists seek to dismantle was built on a dissenting English Protestant foundation. Race, nationality, religion, and language provided a coherence to a society that prized the rule of law, limited government, self-rule in matters of religion and politics, and denominational pluralism, not homogenization, a coherence strengthened by religious-imagery-infused secular arch types concerning a promised land of freedom and well-being. Ideals of universal individual freedom (and Christian pronouncements about all on level ground at the cross) gradually removed race (and ethnicity) as part of the definition of American society.[4]

Religion provided beliefs underlying political principles: the worth and dignity of individuals as God's creatures. Both the founding fathers and later Tocqueville saw the nation's religious faith and political structures as indispensable to one another. Religious words and symbols were used to express a secular faith, not limited (eventually) by the believers' race and nationality, in equality, freedom, justice, and opportunity; these religious words and symbols were the common parlance of political discourse.

What Martin Marty calls "Baptistification" takes place in American religious and secular life: in other words a significant democratization of religious denominations, detectable even in high church, sacramental denominations. The altar call—where the individual of his own volition joins the body of believers—is typically American. Thus, Americans became a nation of collective individualists, says Michael Kammen. People learned to work cooperatively within groups without surrendering individual independence.[5]

Faith and reason came together to create an understanding of the individual as a social and political being. The Judeo-Christian heritage in almost all its variants taught the potential even propensity for evil in every man and woman. The Enlightenment accepted this but reminded the religious that man was created a little less than the angels, crowned with glory, and was granted enough reasoning, awareness, and wisdom to recognize his own proclivities and to set up safeguards against himself and his society so that power could be wielded effectively while its possible abuses were hemmed in and checked.

The nation, North and South, rural and urban, began and remained a capitalist country. Relatively few believed in or sought equality of condition, preferring inequality and liberty. The foundational document of national governmental structure, the Constitution, in order to create a nation at all, denied for a time (until the aftermath of the American Civil War) the ideals of the nation's foundational document of aspirations, the Declaration of Independence, implicitly accepting and protecting human slavery. The nation also began as a patriarchy with women not equal in political rights and not to be equal, some on the Left would say, ever. As from the beginning of civilized life, the foundational social unit of the new nation was not the individual but the family.

Variations on the foundational structures and ideals have made up the internal and foreign policy history of the United States to the present time. The manifest destiny of the City on the Hill is the great overarching myth of the United States. The nation was a new promised land, a righteous empire (as Martin Marty has called it) where democracy and Christianity and capitalism intertwined. The universalist, evangelizing ideology of expansive liberty made it from the start a dangerous nation to the rest of the world's nations of orders and no liberty; it was recognized as such by other national/cultural powers. Evangelical Protestantism united North and South and recurring Awakenings stoked the fires of religious fervency and political/social reform. Lincoln, by his actions and words gave the nation a new birth of freedom and dedication to self-rule. The Republican Party after the Civil War built its political base upon the beliefs and structures and styles of the northern churches. After the passing of the war generation Bryan and then Wilson brought the farther West and the South and the Democratic Party back into the righteous empire. In the late nineteenth and early twentieth centuries in midst of a religious third Awakening, Republicans and Democrats became Progressives looking to enhance and better safeguard democratic rule through various "progressive" measures or ideas, one of which was women's suffrage and another (naively, but perhaps unavoidably given the domestic history of the American people) the exaltation of professionals, technocrats, and bureaucrats, scientific specialists who could rationally assess problems and design solutions. In World War I the United States set out to redeem the world by example and deed and was rebuffed by the old world and the new world of communism, which was full of its own missionary zeal.[6]

At the very moment communism arose to lead all peoples to a man-made heaven on earth, the foundation of American culture was wobbling and shaking. For decades millions of immigrants had been coming to America bringing cultural ideals that had little in common with the traditional culture of their new home. As Richard Hofstadter describes it, the political/social culture of the United States upheld the virtues of abstract law, justice, and independent political action. The new, often non-English speaking arrivals knew none of this; rather they understood the world in terms of personal obligation and loyalty, hierarchy, authority, and group identity and action. The old nation prized pluralism (within Protestantism). Most of the new arrivals saw a Catholic, corporate order; and, at least in the eyes of their religious leaders, any new Protestant promised land was an heretical aberration, a republican land that was to be captured and absorbed into the one true world order ordained by God, theirs.[7]

In time the new millions adapted to the American traditions and amalgamated, the adaptation made all the easier because of voting privileges and well-founded hopes for social/class advancement. Still, their adopted political party, the Democracy, had to give up traditional cultural imagery and words because its southern (Protestant) and northern (Catholic) wings were too far apart culturally to cherish the same imagery and words (all of which, secular or not, derived from Protestantism). Consequently, as Robert Wiebe underlines, the New Deal of the 1930s was truly new in American politics, because it shunned cultural themes (like public schools and prohibition) that had united, but could now divide and concentrated instead on pragmatic money issues. The New Deal also extensively magnified the prestige and power of bureaucratic professionals who labored mightily to restructure the nation's economy and its political values and who now became an interest group of their own within American society.[8]

Pragmatism had already become a topic of great interest and discussion in academic and philosophical circles and among a whole host of progressives who were intent on strengthening a non-religious national order and government. John Dewey had urged that national leaders and academicians not dwell on shoulds and oughts but on the possible, on what can be done, on whatever works to solve problems, suggesting that cultural identities and values were irrelevant or even a hindrance in a new scientific age.[9]

Pragmatists, the more liberal social gospelers, and the irreligious as early as the years right after America's crusade to save the world in the Great War (1914–1918) seemed for quite a while to have gained an upper hand in national politics with Protestants and Catholics in stalemate. Cynicism, such as H L. Mencken's, directed at the "boobocracy" and religion seemed to be the rage of a new era with the Scopes Monkey Trial and Clarence Darrow's mocking of the old, middle-class, Protestant standard-bearer, Bryan. Some Americans, looking to communism, rejected both the old culture and cynicism and hoped for a non-religious, more compassionate, more just world, trusting in technology/science and pragmatism and benefiting from recent history's cultural fragmentation. The old religion was not gone but would rise again in power (aided at times by amalgamated Catholics) in the latter part of the twentieth century, at the same time as the rise of the Secular Ideologues as the latest manifestation of devout Secularists.

As noted above, compounding this post-World War I disruption in traditional order was the rise of a communist party within the United States, what historians now call the Old Left. For some citizens the inequalities and injustices within the nation, especially regarding class and race, were too much to bear. According to communist dogma the capitalist based, republican government always served those who profited from the work of others and it seemed to such citizens that those others, those laborers, always struggled to survive. Communism seemed to some, then, a coherent ideology with a certainty (historical determinism) of success. It offered compassion for the dispossessed, hope for the future, and incredible faith in man's own capacity for improvement and perfection.

The adjective "incredible" is used here because communist apologists never offered a satisfactory explanation of how a morally good being could have ever been corrupted in the first place and would avoid being corrupted again once the evils of property, capital, and religion had been removed. Nevertheless, because of such faith the great American Protestant theologian, Reinhold Niebuhr, who insisted on man's imperfectability as a constant, used early Common Era Jewish and Christian terminology when calling communists children of light—as opposed to those of darkness, the fascists, who placed no hope in the individual man. Whatever their beliefs, or perhaps because of the desperate need to believe in a coming millennium so great as to justify all the means taken to get there, American communists followed unquestioningly the directives of the Soviet Union. They supported or opposed the American political establishment as diplomacy and war in Europe dictated, never wondering about the millions murdered in the Soviet Union as the communist vanguard led people forward to a new, better day. American communists were very few in number, but they provided an intellectual, ideological framework for an alternative America, a framework that has had impact down to the present day, including on the part of some an automatic self-criticism of American failings. Self-criticism of the United States would not necessarily distinguish communists in their righteous indignation from that of Jews or Christians, except for communism's premise that man is a god lacking tragic flaws.[10]

It is the whole question of personal humility, grounded in a Judeo-Christian sense of tragedy, not history's progress or determinism, that provides the United States its greatest distinction from communism/secularism. Niebuhr addresses this issue in his *Children of Light and Children of Darkness*. The United States has rejected all efforts to find cultural unity by ending religious diversity. It had until the 1960s refused to disavow traditional historical religions and the roots secular institutions have in those religions. Quoting Niebuhr:

> The fact is that a theory of democratic toleration which enjoins provisional freedom for all religious in the hope that the bourgeois climate of opinion will gradually dissipate all religious convictions except the secularized bourgeois versions of them, is a typical fruit of the illusions of modern "children of light." They expect modern society to achieve an essential uniformity through the common convictions of "men of good-will" who have been enlightened by modern liberal education. This belief fails to appreciate the endless variety of cultural and religious convictions, growing out of varying historical situations. It does not understand the perennial power of particularity in human culture. . . . The creed is . . . dangerous because no society, not even a democratic one, is great enough or good enough to make itself the final end of human existence. In its more sophisticated form secularism represents a form of skepticism which is conscious of the relativity of all human perspectives. In this form it stands on the abyss of moral nihilism and threatens the whole of life with a sense of meaninglessness. Thus it creates a spiritual vacuum into which demonic religions easily rush. . . . The solution [to all this] . . . demands that each religion . . . seek to proclaim its highest insights while yet preserving an humble and contrite recognition of the fact that all expressions of religious faith are subject to historical contingency and relativity. Such a recognition creates a spirit of tolerance. . . .[11]

Lincoln, with his words of truth, judgment, mercy, and humility, is the nation's best example of this in a secular leader. His words, or words like them, uttered today by a political leader would be understood by Secular Ideologues as frightening, liberty-threatening incantations.

After World War II, when the evangelizing communists and capitalists had walked with the devil (each other) to get across the bridge (to defeat fascism), the differing evangelicals parted ways and resumed their separate efforts to win the world. In early 1947, with the Soviet Union controlling all of Eastern Europe and attempting to control the Bosporus and Greece, the President stated in his Truman Doctrine that the United States would support free people resisting subjugation. Then in June 1947 the administration announced the Marshall Plan of economic assistance to Western Europe to stave off a possible domestic communist rise to power. In 1948, Henry Wallace ran for President on the Progressive Party ticket, appealing to old Leftists and campaigning against Truman for not having been diplomatic enough with the Soviet Union, a charge similar to those that would later be made against President Bush and his war on terrorism.

At the same time, despite its own civil liberties failings, indeed, because of its awareness of them, the United States, opting to keep its traditional culture, moved forward again toward greater justice for racial minorities. Franklin Roosevelt during World War II issued regulations to offer African-Americans greater opportunities for federal war contracts and/or jobs. Truman and Eisenhower integrated the armed forces. Eisenhower used the military to enforce court-ordered school integration. Kennedy and Johnson pursued passage of anti-discrimination civil rights laws. Nixon promulgated the regulations that laid down guidelines for affirmative action for both minorities and females (who had gained suffrage rights in 1920) and initiated an all voluntary military that opened more opportunities for women in military services.

NEW CONSTRUCTS

Life as people had known it was changing in many ways. Unknown to Americans at the time those living in the 1950s were living in the last decade of family stability. The percent of people in marriages would never be as high again. The percent of unwed births never as low. The percent of marriages ending in divorce never as low.[12]

While all this was going on a New Left in American politics arose, drawing much of its strength first from anger over the Vietnam War, second from rage over domestic social injustices, and third from a youthful desire to reject "the establishment" (meaning in this instance a man-made social and economic system that constricted individual actions and exploited the natural world). They wanted to replace it with one in which the earth and people were in communion and people more in touch with their "natural selves." Its members were literally and figuratively the children of the Old Left. They admired and romanticized some of the world's nationalist/communist insurrectionist leaders but were not necessarily communist themselves. They never consciously recognized the inherent contradiction between communism's "scientific" foundation and ways and their own deep romanticism. Perhaps this is so because, like fascism and communism, science and romanticism eventually converge to create dreams of a utopian brave new world.

Differing from the Old, the New Left did not necessarily adhere, however, to an orthodox ideology that saw historical determinism as a foundation for an eventual new world order: rather it wanted the benefits of the millennium now in terms of freedom from restraint of any kind. The New Left was about finding one's true self and expressing one's true self. It tended toward anarchy and the individual libertine, especially in matters of sexual and drug exploration and experimentation. As a movement, the New Left dissipates with the end of the Vietnam War and the end of the draft and the fading away of many New Left sympathizers who were moving out of the role and status of college student into that of job holders, some becoming professors and news editors.

Out of this dissipation of the New Left a still newer Left, the Secular Ideologues, emerged, not so much energized at first by an ongoing war but by dreams of individual freedom that had been given more focus by the nonmajoritarian courts and executive-bureaucracy-driven civil rights movement and by a developing ideology of relativism and antimajoritarianism, which was in part itself a residue of war cynicism. As with the preceding New Left, there are no card-carrying members and no one detailing or enforcing a confession. There is, though, a commonly held orthodoxy made up of: various intertwined threads of American history referenced already (and to be referenced later), the Old and New Left's great desire to tear down and start over, and the earlier groups' unquestioning faith in their own vision and morality. It is incoherent and self-contradictory in many places, but all thoughts and ideals of the Secular Ideologues are subsumed under the aspiration to dismantle the foundations of the old culture to transform their dream of self-expression into reality and to construct new power loci to safeguard true freedom. Perhaps seeing themselves like the old communist vanguard, the movement's devotees, many of whom are literary intellectuals and academics, have no problem drawing wages from the operations of the corrupt, chafing republican/capitalist system and the taxes of the less free, less enlightened citizens of that system, some of whom (i.e. unreconstructed men) must be pushed aside. Most certainly, like the old vanguard, Secular Ideologues really do not trust "the people's" ability to see the truth as well as they—hence their impatience with democratic legislatures and constitutional/cultural checks and balances.

Early twentieth century British Christian apologist G. K. Chesterton once referred to the United States as a nation with the soul of a church. The condition of that soul had become far more precarious after 1960 as the United States was pulled by the Secularists down a path already taken by Europe.[13]

By the twenty-first century once common and expected public expressions of religious faith and the framing of community and community challenges inside religious tenets, traditions, and ethics had become a deep affront to Secularists. Secularists constantly denounced President George W. Bush for his public references to God, religion, and prayer. Ralph Nader denounced Bush for such words and deeds, finding him abhorrent and saying the country should have only a truly secular President. Professor Martha C. Nussbaum in her *Liberty of Conscience* continually blasts President Bush for public prayer as offensive to non-Christians and even finds offensive any references to a Protestant Christian heritage. Campaigning for the Presidency, Obama lamented the need of people on the political right to find comfort in guns and religion and in his inaugural said it was time to put away childish things and be pragmatic.[14]

Modernization had taken its toll. All "progress" was not a blessing. Protestantism in a democracy like the United States tends sooner or later to no mystery in faith, greater rationality, and less devoutness, all for the sake of equality and/or personal freedom and/or material well-being. Europeans had cut the religious roots that had held them down, becoming, of course, rootless, and then seeking a new grounding in fascism or communism. Others had remained rootless, intellectually ethereal, physically-fixated libertines. Still others had sought not independence but security in secular socialism. In Europe typically the government portion of the gross national product has been until now far greater than in the United States. France's President, Nicolas Sarkozy, has described his nation's faith as "secular fundamentalism."[15]

In the United States, the philosophical, theological, ideological appeals of modern Europe were always there, especially attractive to the nation's intelligentsia and posers. The effects of this appeal were magnified by what occurred after 1960. In the 1960s the people of the United States separated into two divergent cultural camps, Traditionalists and Secularists, a division that is wider than anything Americans had experienced since the Civil War. Until the 1960s, most Americans, Democrats or Republicans, rich or poor, white or of color, male or female, Protestants, Catholics, or Jews all had had a common understanding that there was a moral order to the universe that provided people with values and a sense of right and wrong. Many Europeans had already left behind this universe and now Americans will too. One cannot be free if constrained by such standards; one cannot fully experience their own individuality. This is, of course, the primordial clash of order and chaos or the ever-repeating Hebraic story of the Fall of Man. This latest manifestation has deeply divided Americans from then to now. On one side is an understanding of human kind in terms of tragedy and grace and on the other a vision of, and devout belief in, limitless individualism.[16]

In his *The Enemy at Home*, Dinesh D'Souza makes the critically important point that the moral divide centers on religion and family and is reflected in political party positions. Most Evangelicals, churchgoing Catholics and Orthodox Jews vote Republican. Secularists vote overwhelmingly Democratic. D'Souza quotes Clinton pollster Dick Morrison: "If a woman is divorced, she is almost certain to be a Democrat. If she's single, she is likely to lean Democratic. If she's married, she's likely to lean Republican. If she's married with children, she's safely in the Republican camp."[17]

After 1960, visible, tangible moorings to the traditional floated away. Women went to work outside the home in far greater numbers than ever before. Meanwhile, non-skilled men were losing their jobs, and manufacturing jobs went into long-term decline while service and bureaucratic jobs, including those of colleges and universities soared. America had fully entered the post-industrial age. People lost a sense of connection with the earth (hence flower children's seeking out the mythical Earth Goddess) and the material world where everything came from, since most people knew no one who dug anything out of the ground or molded raw materials into goods needed or desired by others. Blue collar unions gave way to pink collar unions often made up of governmental employees, especially women. Electricity was the product of a switch and milk was something made in some distant factory. Pushing paper and typing on keyboards, Americans had lost a sense of work and its dignity and creativity (there sits the house I built, or there sits the train car of coal I loaded). In a very real sense they had lost their grounding.

Marxists and other "for the people" academics were living very well off the work and taxes of people they really did not know (or like), people who wanted, not their ideas or help, but a sense of vitality tied to work. By the twenty-first century the well-to-do urbanites and the richest Americans, almost all laboring in bureaucratic environments, were voting Democratic while the less well-to-do people were voting Republican.[18]

Most critical in all this, men lost their sense of purpose as men. David Blankenhorn sees the nation's most critical problem as fatherlessness. Blankenhorn sees a powerful, hugely influential, intellectual and cultural elite that is determined to remove the concept of fatherhood from the public mind. Sometime in the late twentieth century, says Blankenhorn, a goodly number of Americans quit believing in the necessity or even the desirability of fatherhood.

Intellectually, the idea of superfluous fatherhood rests on three propositions. The first is that fatherhood as a gender-based social role is literally what the dictionary defines as superfluous: exceeding what is necessary. The second proposition is that men in general, and fathers in particular, are part of the problem. The third is that social progress depends largely upon a transformation of fatherhood based on the ideal of gender role convergence. Secularists objected to the very idea of paternal identity, the transfer of gender identity to children. No longer was human completion seen as two complimentary sexes. Rather completion was found in actual mental and physical androgyny. Here is the triumph of the Secularists' radical individualism. And apparently that individualism can go yet further. In Europe's France, Spain, and Portugal citizens are so insistent on the abandonment of social mores, perhaps in reaction to long histories of corporatism and later fascism, that they place no community restrictions on consenting adult incest.[19]

Blankenhorn sees this historical phenomenon as extraordinarily destructive of culture and civilization. No longer was dad expected to do, to provide, to

protect, to live a certain life, and by doing all this to sponsor/confirm and pre-
pare the young for the future through character modeling and development.
Most devastating in all this, Secularists had denied one of the dominant ideas
of the Judeo-Christian tradition, that of servanthood and the acceptance of
responsibility. All this, says Blankenhorn, leads not to fulfillment but narcis-
sism and hostility to larger social goals. In other words, when the community
quits socializing boys into men, civilization teeters on the eternal abyss. In
the Unites States by 1986 for the first time ever, a majority of poor families
had no fathers, expanding the number of "fatherless boys [who] commit
crimes."[20]

This explains the ensuing rootlessness and forlornness of America's Secular Ideologues. Bill Bishop in his *The Big Sort: Why the Clustering of Like-
Minded America Is Tearing Us Apart* examines the thoughts and theories of
linguist George Lakoff (traditionalist America, for Lakoff, is freedom denying) who sees the post 1960s United States divided between two very different social systems based on two very different kinds of families, one headed
by a strict father and the other by a "nurturant parent." The first emphasizes
rules and authority as necessary for self-reliance and good character. The
second stresses love and empathy producing healthy and fulfilled offspring.
Bishop recounts that two political scientists at the University of Michigan
tested Lakoff's theory that the two value sets determined political conservatism and liberalism. The large-scale study showed that views on child rearing
and fatherhood were a stronger indicator of party affiliation than income.
Americans no longer agreed about their most basic values. Giving a personal
example of how Americans segregated themselves almost automatically along
this fault line, Bishop described his home town in Texas as having an area of
far more liberal people, and one of far more Traditionalists, both areas with
churches that held socials that defined them as different. The Traditionalists
all brought food for everyone and mingled. The Secularist families brought
food only for their own consumption and ate separately from one another. In
other words community at the most elemental level had become only a word
with no real meaning behind it.[21]

As Niebuhr said long ago a great risk of nihilism is present here, as Europe
found out before World War II and has continued finding out ever since.
Somewhere inside themselves America's not-yet-jaded Secularists seek to
avoid their fate by living within their particular paradox, that of being at one
and the same time both extreme individualists and tribesmen. The old, traditional home is no more. In fact some disdain the heritage. But aloneness is
intolerable for most, and the need to be part of something and some enterprise
beyond one's self is almost universal. Hence, the Secularists identity with race
and/or ethnic groups and/or gender and/or ideological groupings that vigor-

ously attack the old, while defending the prerogatives of the individual and hence the ironic group-think and the closing of the American mind on university campuses that have become fortresses for a new right (i.e. correct)—thinking order. Also, like Parisians of the French Revolution and the later European communists, the Secularists support Rousseau's General Will expressed through a powerful, pragmatic-posing government set free of all the cultural values of the old order and of all the subordinate social/political groupings of the old order that gave people multiple identities and strengths outside that of the central governmental power.

AN AMALGAMATION OF GROUP ANARCHISTS

What makes their own self-absorption and pride (that they are wiser and free of the will to power) less recognizable to them is that many, if not most, genuinely have empathy for those oppressed in any manner and seek redress of various societal evils. The ideology can best be understood by looking at how it takes ideals and values of the old order, retaining the value-laden words of the old order, but infusing them with new meaning and then applying the old words with new meanings to various present-day political and social topics such as: race/ethnic relations; feminism; education; gay rights; family; multiculturalism; internationalism; and religion in public life.

So Secularists pour new wine into old skins hoping for a freedom that can only be achieved by a significant restructuring of what anthropologists refer to as the three foundational pillars of any civilization: government, religion, and perhaps the most fundamental of all, family. For the Secularists that new freedom is dependent upon a dismantling of the old WASP (white Anglo-Saxon Protestant) world and a dethroning of the straight, white, Protestant male, the acknowledged and vilified common enemy of all those seeking greater freedom through a new, better vision of American life as seen through the multiple prisms of the categories referenced in the preceding paragraph. Thus the cultural war's multiple battle fronts: white versus non-white in race relations; men versus women in gender relations and educational philosophy and testing; straights versus gays; patriarchs versus democratic, caring families with men optional; the patriotism of the old order versus multiculturalism; freedom to be one person in both private and public life versus the banishment of religion-infused personal life from the public square.

The Secularists' clothing of new ideals in old words is perhaps best and most easily seen in its understanding and arguments for racial justice. The nation had sought to improve employment and educational opportunities for its racial minorities. It had done so by paying attention to race when awarding governmental contracts and admitting youth into colleges and professional schools. People had to be identified by what they were, what they were born as. Furthermore, people were identified as what they were not—white, as in the old people and their old ways. Almost immediately after passage of the 1964 Civil Rights Act governmental bureaucrats, part of the technocracy so trusted by both Republican and Democratic reformers in the twentieth century, exercised their extraordinary strength to go so far as to successfully defy the non-discriminatory language of the 1964 law by insisting that affirmative action programs *insure* an end result. The benefits of American society were to be proportioned out on the basis of race/ethnicity. Accordingly, Lani Guinier, Bill Clinton's first nominee for Director of the Justice Department's Civil Rights Division, resurrected John C. Calhoun's concurrent majority theory, designed by him to protect the slave owning minority section of the nation, proposing ways (such as super majorities) for various minorities to have a veto over normal majoritarian legislation and thus provide leverage insuring proportional benefits. In the name of equality the Secular Left was now pursuing an ideal of group entitlement.[22]

Words lost their meaning. The United States Supreme Court in its *United Steel Workers of America* v. *Weber* case supported the ideas behind the bureaucracy's actions, ruling that in order for the government to ensure true opportunity and equality it was reasonable to go knowingly beyond the words and the documented intent of the 1964 Civil Rights Act forbidding favoritism, so far beyond in fact that favoritism was legal! Not surprisingly one state government boldly asserted in its welfare cabinet's affirmative action plan that it would pursue a *nondiscriminatory employment policy of having a twenty percent minority and seventy-five percent female workforce*. Any common understanding of the rule of law created by the majority and of the actual words in the law was crumbling.[23]

All of this applied to affirmative action for females. A loss in meaning, in terms of words and human relationships, has been one result of women's drive to be all that they could be. The United State's Supreme Court's *Roe* decision confirmed a right to an abortion that did not exist in the Constitution, abrogating all laws passed by duly elected legislative bodies. Majoritarianism is not an ideal of the newest Left. The arguments for right to privacy and abortion undercut all arguments for statutory rape laws. Men had no say in an abortion decision and no say in child support. Women are discriminated against in pay not because of pay differentials between the sexes for the same jobs, but because women sometimes choose (because of male established social expectations) lower paying jobs and/or careers. Accordingly, a governmental technocracy is needed to override the market place, determine what constitutes equal work among different tasks, jobs, and professions across the nation, and then order compensation.[24]

Ultimately there has to be a new sexual relationship with men if there is to be true equality between males and females—it is preferable to use the words male and female, like the military, instead of man and woman, because the former are more clinical and scientific than the latter which can more easily imply an intimacy and interconnectedness beyond the test tube and DNA. On the other hand, any expansive and overarching relationship supposedly defined by biology is rejected. As David Blankenhorn has noted in his *Fatherless America* "our elite culture has now fully incorporated in its prevailing family narrative the idea that fatherhood, as a distinctive social role for men, is either unnecessary or undesirable." On this issue the Newest Left rejects even the Truth of Science mantra, as illustrated by the brouhaha over former Harvard President Summers' comments about most men and women perhaps thinking differently, as almost all scientific studies suggest.[25]

The Secular Ideologues not only ignore their roots in rationalism here but also their competing roots in romanticism. They reject their ties to Mother Nature and insist that nature is not destiny. All gender roles, according to stalwart feminists, are social—unless referring to evil men—and can be restructured. A romanticized view of mankind's rational powers sets in—much like Old Communists in this regard. Men can be taught to be less competitive, more cooperative, less aggressive, less possessive, more communal, more sharing, both in society at large and inside marriages. Or, if not, except for test tube inseminations, they can be pushed outside society. One can only hope, it is supposed, that the condition and the cure do not turn the nation into *A Clock Work Orange* society. Whatever, men need to be trained to take care of homes and children, but definitely not women. Failing that or until such time that men's transformation is a reality, retired Brandeis professor Linda Heischman has urged that women marry feminists or marry down and limit themselves to one child. Today secular European relativists, seeking all they can be and have, are limiting themselves as couples to one child and in the process, as George Weigel points out, are committing cultural suicide by failing to create future generations.[26]

Abortion is the most critical of all feminist issues because it frees women from nature, free to be separate from men and/or more like them. Extreme situations are used to justify and camouflage an exercise in convenience for freedom's sake. As so well noted by Allen Bloom, abortion as a right meant women gave up modesty and in so doing surrendered their control of serious intimate sexual relations.[27]

At the same time women took off in two very different directions. In one direction lay "free sex." Women were now like men. For Secularists, sex, like religion, became a thing unto itself, not a pervasive influence across one's life, but a part, a segment to be enjoyed for itself, not necessarily a tie to long-lasting intimacy with anyone. Of course all the passion was gone. Again, as Bloom has noted, sex as an end unto itself subdued intellectual passion and inquisitiveness on America's campuses. Once, the drive for sex, its passion and the fulfillment in another it could lead to, had been intertwined with a young person's intellectual curiosity and awakening. Now sex had become passé and enlightenment a ho-hum enterprise. The great tiger behind the door had emerged as a tabby.[28]

In the other direction lay a world of "sex! What sex? There better not be any sex!" The workplace had to be free of sexual harassment if there was to be true equal opportunity, not tempered by intimidation. Academic professors and newspaper essayists, whose work was done mostly in isolation, imagined, sought, and insisted on a work world where there was no talk, hints, or suggestions of men and women related by sex drives, so much so that all sexual banter, compliments, courtesies had to be abolished. Flirtations, no matter how free of aggression or oppression, as opposed to ogling, manhandling, or ugly words, had to be formally removed from the work environment. Women who often worked alone imagined that women and men who daily worked side by side wanted (at least the women) a world where the two sexes related to one another only by the social tasks they shared. They would be automations with no other draw between them. One could almost see the gray and brown walls of communist Moscow and East Berlin.

Of course the problem is that some have figured out that if sex is a thing separate from all else, then the two feminist paths can come full circle and merge. Neither path offers a vision of sex as being vital to civilization's social structure. One can work as if sex does not exist and play like it does. All this is a dance around the obvious: that in the natural world, unless there is a sexual draw and relationship above and beyond job titles and functions, there will not be any more men and women. In their drive to be free of men, feminists have not only given up modesty, they have laid down their power to draw, hold, and build and to fire creative inspiration with laughter.

Other more radical feminists have identified a third way. Men are not only unnecessary but too fundamentally flawed to fool with. All the perceived evils of western and American civilization are male. There can be no sufficient social restructuring: "men, can't live with them." There is no corollary of "Can't live without them." For these women all sexual relations with men are forms of male aggression and are oppressive. Accordingly, a feminist professor at Harvard would not let men in her class, and a long ago Bryn Mawr educator in referring to the school's female student body, would remark that "Our failures marry."[29]

The great feminist war for more self-actualization somewhere became a war against men more than it was a war for freedom and equality. Educational reforms of the last four decades clearly indicate this. Educational directors and reformers in the United States sought the advancement of women by straight-arming and holding back men by hyping spurious gender myths and by intentionally designing reforms that shuffled male students into corners.

In the 1960s and 1970s the World War II generation sent its children to college. They had no gender agendas and sent both their sons and daughters. The Nixon administration included women in affirmative action guidelines. Within a generation women made up at least fifty percent of the medical and law school enrollments and continued to totally dominate the increasingly influential and economically and politically powerful educational and nursing professions. Far more females were graduating from high school and far more women than men were going to college and graduating. This has been a well-documented worldwide phenomenon.

Nevertheless, feminist academicians did undocumented—[so much for scientific method]—studies saying that during all this time women were behind in education and called for reforms. The reforms included: no recess; less individual attainment and more group studies and achievement; special programs for girls to learn more math and science; no such programs for boys to read and write better; special programs for girls to learn leadership and none for boys; government-sponsored college internships for girls, not boys (at least not white boys); math tests designed to measure written explanations of answers that gave credit even when the answer was wrong and gave only partial credit for right answers with poorly written addenda; an increase of testing for writing on college entrance tests and a co-terminus reduction of testing for math logic.[30]

With more attention girls, who always did better in reading and writing, caught up and surpassed boys in math/science testing while boys, with no assistance in reading and writing (or math and science) remained far behind girls in this area. High schools and colleges have been graduating classes with almost all academic and campus activity awards going to women. Boys get sports awards. Compounding this problem was a feminist insistence for much of the last forty years that men and women, boys and girls, thought processes were the same. There is an irony here since this would imply that all those evil men had been socialized to be that way by their mothers who in turn had already been socialized to be almost the only nurturers children had.

There are more ironies. Feminists have resisted all suggestions that some boys and girls may do better if taught separately in public schools and have insisted on the end of all men's campuses. But they have fought hard to retain women only colleges. In just the last couple of years some women's colleges have had to start accepting boys to remain financially solvent because of fall-ing women's enrollment numbers. Apparently many women were not inter-ested in the new sexual war. The men were enticed not by academics, but the chance to play ball and probably by the presence of a whole lot of women.

Clearly the agenda of the Secular Ideologues is not just about self-real-ization and equality for all, but is also about a tearing down of traditional structures and values and even men generally, anything they view as standing in their way. Internal ideological consistency does not exist and is not dealt with, only the drive to be unrestrained and to tear down. Loudness and fury on several fronts maintains the ideological drive by holding inconsistencies together unexamined and by covering up a core of egotism with explications of traditional injustices that inflict personal pain. One of the greatest ironies facing the Secularists, one that they refuse to address, is that life can only be rationalized or reasoned out so far and that sometimes two goods can clash and there will be pain and there can be no complete resolution. In other words, ideology can only carry an individual so far and, if the individual does not realize this, it will carry him/her away, like the hero of Warren Beatty's classic movie *REDS*.

Perhaps the one issue, the one ideological value most illustrative of this irony is that of gay rights. Here there is deep personal pain. Here there are great clashes of values held by the Secular Ideologues. And here the intensity of the clash between Traditionalists and Secularists is intense, second only to the war over religion, to which the dispute over gay rights is intrinsically connected. Over a decade ago, Canadian lesbian lawyer Barbara Finlay saw that "the legal struggle for queer rights will one day be a struggle between freedom of religion versus sexual orientation." Actually, today the Tradition-alist have already lost the war in Canada and Europe where laws prohibit "hate language" from Christian conservatives.[31]

Intriguingly, determined feminists have vigorously opposed heterosexual pornography but not gay pornography. Gay pornography is not male objec-tification of women, no diminution, no lesser than. With gay pornography there is no power struggle. But if sex is only a thing unto itself, not something pointing to a pervasive reality across all of one's life, can there be any objec-tification by anyone? Why pay any mind to any kind of pornography at all?

More confusing still, in that part of the Secular Ideologue world in which males are not identified as inherently evil, heterosexual roles and relation-ships are axiomatically social constructs not biological ones. Yet, setting aside the libertine, the jaded, the abused, and the gender isolated, in that same world homosexual roles and relationships are axiomatically biological. No straight man is allowed to claim that he can be naked with naked women and have no serious problem with desire. Few straight men would wish to make such a claim. Yet, so that all can be treated the same, as in the armed forces, gay men make that claim about themselves and naked men, and are supported in this claim by Secular Ideologues, even though the gay argument is that they are no different from straights, with all the same drives and desires except for the object of desire. The same example and analogies apply for lesbians. Outside a twenty-four hour a day feminist, asexual work place, there is no reconciling this clash of sexual drive and individual equality of treatment in all circumstances.

This question of social roles gets even thornier when one looks at that primary building block, as anthropologists tell us, of all civilizations—the family. Family here means the bond between a man and a woman that produces children and the woman's hold on a man through sex (meaning far more than the act itself) and/or children that maintains a union and may cause a man (especially) or woman to seek the welfare of others beyond themselves. Can there be other families? Yes, but not with the same primordial purpose.

Traditionalists argue that children do better with mother and father role models. Though they do not always attack this position head-on, as they do with other issues, this is really intolerable for Secular Ideologues. A father role, a mother role, whatever they might be, suggest there are biological/natural distinctions, not socially constructed. This flies in the face of the core belief of the Secular Existentialists that they can cut themselves off from nature and the past and start anew. They support gay marriage and adoption, so that gays desirous of doing so are not denied the social status and equality and comfort legally and emotionally of creating families, sometimes arguing that gay parents could not be any worse than many heterosexual parents—an argument that actually leads away from the issue at hand. But if there are father and mother roles arising out of biology, then the heterosexual drive for family (and the resulting civilization) cannot be fully reconciled with the homosexual, and very human, natural, need to belong, which is a greater need than the legal one.[32]

Actually, most experts agree that two married biological parents are best for children and that marriage is beneficial for both men and women. Still political correctness runs through the social sciences. For most of the last four decades of the twentieth century, the idea or ideal of a stay-at-home mom did not exist in school family studies textbooks. Following a European lead—the 2000 European Union' Charter of Fundamental Rights does not include a right to family as natural or fundamental—American constitutional historian Martha Nussbaum argues that family is a creation of the state and thus can be whatever the state says it is.[33]

On the social left something of the mother role remains, but many there no longer desire any father role. Such Secularists reject traditional Biblical presentations of human nature as involving complimentary and completing sexes, believing instead "that human completion is a solo act." [34]

The issues of race, gender, gender-preference positioned as antagonistic offspring of traditional society inevitably creates yet another broad discordant theme: multiculturalism. Like the earlier discussed issues, the multicultural-ism of the Secularists has been created by their intertwining of several tra-ditional threads or values to create a new thing. These values include a con-siderable tolerance for others and their ways and thoughts, respect for others different from you, the right to freedom, the value of pluralism.

The development of particular civil rights tools and objectives in the late twentieth century made the creation of a peculiar American multicul-turalism necessary. As noted earlier, the goals of affirmative action had become almost immediately quotas necessitating not just correct, legal ac-tion but outcomes determined not by ability but by gender or race. When the majoritarian public became increasingly intolerant of such preferential treatment, affirmative action shaded into Supreme Court Justice Powell's lone argument in Bakke for a university's right to seek diversity as part of a learning experience. Diversity, as Peter Wood notes, made the incredible and false argument that by definition people of different colors or ethnicity came from different cultures with different thoughts and values and that the mixing of these different cultures by mixing colors was good. Culture was a codeword really for racial/ethnic groupings, not different ways of think-ing or different value sets. Heterogeneous populations were such a positive good that homogeneity in thoughts and values, at least when talking about traditional culture, was bad and amalgamation into that culture was bad. As one professor has stated, amalgamation robs both the nation and those new immigrants of a different culture and consequently as many languages as possible should be preserved and taught so as to keep everyone different. The professor evidenced no concern about the values of any introduced culture that might clash with republicanism and the ideals of the Declara-tion of Independence. Supposed, but not necessarily actual, differences in group cultures or subcultures had to be maintained to impart strength to a new non-national civilization where everyone came together as separatists because they were different (a grand contradiction of anthropological, and historical evidence) and to maintain the distinctiveness of imagined diver-sified groups in order to continue providing the individual the freedoms, prerogatives, and preferences he/she is entitled to. Thus the great insistence of Secularists—despite the Old Testament warning story of Babel—that the nation be and forever remain at least bilingual.[35]

This is not to say that a great many sub-cultural differences should not be cherished. The nation does not need to rid itself of Cajun food, Mountain songs, Delta blues, Native American tribal customs, or Chinatowns. But for a true civilization to survive there must be overarching myths that point to universally understood and accepted ultimate values expressed in a commonly understood way. The Secular Ideologues reject this because they want their cultural groupings, fictitious or not, precisely because they can serve as fortresses for special privilege—and as such impediments to any cultural or political cohesiveness as one people, a social structure that would by their definition smother individualism.

Multiculturalists seek an amalgamation of group anarchists, a unity found in granting everyone and all groups freedom of self-expression not bounded by any commonly accepted values (which are relative anyway) other than granting all their right to find their own truth. Consequently it must reject the traditional American and western cultures (and the *relatively* greater freedoms they sustain) and what they see as those cultures' restrictive, intolerant, and enslaving values, especially regarding race/gender freedoms. As Jeffrey Hart writes, "the villain always turns out to be variously white, male, Western, racist, imperialist, sexist, or homophobic—or, with any luck, all of them together." The United States is attacked from within by the Secular Ideologues for being a bastion of old, Western ideals and for preferring those ideals, while the rest of the world's civilizations and cultures are held up as all of equal worth (one dare not be intolerant, especially when there are no absolutes) and superior to the United States (apparently because the United States is intolerant). The irony here is so profound as to reach the realm of absurdity for, quoting Hart again:

> . . . it is obvious nonsense to say that they are all equal, or equally desirable. In fact, Multiculturalism is a purely Western invention. . . . None of the cultures we are supposed to be "multi" about is at all itself multicultural. . . . In fact, multiculturalism is an ideological academic fantasy maintained in bad faith. It really amounts to a form of anti-Westernism.[36]

Multiculturalism explains the internationalist posture of the Secular Ideologues. Their internal approach to American culture and power is reproduced on the world stage. Every nation (and its culture) has equal standing with every other nation and culture regardless of internal politics or ideals. All nations must act to pursue their own self-interest (self expression writ really large), especially in relation to the United States. The United States is again the exception. Its culture and ideals are not good, and it *should* refrain from exercising power. Other countries (as with internal separate cultures) acting in concert through the United Nations and through non-elected world courts (again like internal Secular politics) must hem in and reduce the United

States. According to Samuel Huntington this is a common and consistent theme preached on universities across the nation.[37]

The Secular Ideologues see and forgive (or at least ignore) and often defend other nations' drives for power—it is much like their own drives for self-expression—just not that of the United States. All United States' actions must be peaceful and then presumably others, free of unjust restraint, would be peaceful, a truly incredible assumption. From Vietnam on, all manifestations of the Left have sought to restrain American military power. Neither having nor desiring any sense of history, except when it fits their ideology, history is rewritten when necessary to justify present political positions or to create heroes for the cause as, for example, one university professor's recasting of World War II and Cold War Warrior John F. Kennedy as a leader the exact opposite of today's bad or unhealthy leadership, a man who spoke not of fear but hope, not of war but peace. Kennedy did indeed speak of hope and peace, but never did he suggest either was a reality or could be a reality outside American military strength and the willingness to use it.[38]

Some on the left have called for unilateral disarmament. One sincere Ideologue, aghast at the present destruction in the world and America's part in that destruction has written:

> We cannot get rid of violence by perpetrating violence. That is sheer folly. To attempt this, one must be very unwise, insane or a criminal. Or all of the above. . . . Therefore, the way to change the world is by being a model. . . . If the United States wants to see a nuclear-free world, we are going to have to disarm ourselves. . . . We will create a peaceful and secure world by inviting the international community to follow our lead in eliminating weapons stockpiles . . . violent means have been nothing but complete failures regarding long-term desirable ends.

The Secular Ideologues insist on a diplomacy for the United States alone that is divorced from power considerations, that ignores the dictum that war is diplomacy by other means and Jesus's parable of war lords measuring the cost and benefits of war. The person quoted above cited Ghandi as an example to emulate; he did not cite Jesus, perhaps because the Romans' actions may have brought into question his assumption about everyone's willingness to follow men of peace. The Secular Ideologues, like the Old Left, trusting in the basic goodness of man—except for the exceptional bad guys overwhelmed by power and selfishness that must themselves be overcome—strongly argue for a form of diplomacy separated from considerations of assertions, or possible assertions, of power. France, Germany and Russia acted reasonably to protect their money and/or geopolitical national interests in the drive up to war with Iraq. The United States, in not forswearing its own interests, acted unreasonably and out of control. Thus, the failure of prewar and wartime diplomacy.[39]

The Secularists damn the United States for a reality of human nature and national relations that cannot be fixed. They reject in their personal lives, in their nation's culture and in international affairs the inevitability of the drive for power. This is their grand illusion and greatest self-deception. They do not see that their own pursuit of self-expression and freedom from restraint does not necessarily bring justice or peace, but will inevitably devolve into pride and the pursuit of power as an end in itself. So long as they can loudly rail against the great enemy of true freedom, they can hide from themselves the fact that tragedy is inescapable. It is unlikely that the Secular Ideologues ponder that Western word tragedy, its meaning, manifestations, and ramifications. Understandably, they reject both the study of their nation's history (except to identify past evil and excise it from the present) and the old religion that warns them about themselves; they push on to their own vision of the Elysian Fields. Having thrown out and away the old white men of the past, they do not have Shakespeare (or Freud or so many others) warning them that human destiny seems caught up forever in overcoming one's self, one's very nature, and in finding at one and the same time life and freedom *both* in and separate from the older generation.[40]

So great is their need to overthrow, the Secularists at the present moment in the worldwide cultural war cannot grasp that there is such a war. Peace is the absence of American assertions of interests or will. Consequently nothing is said about the world's cultures that reject as godless and heinous multiculturalism and secularism and any definition of freedom that the Ideologues formulate. Somehow this will all be overcome if these others are free to be all they can be. But, "then, as the gay-bar owners are discovering in a fast-Islamifying Amsterdam, reality reasserts itself." The failure of fervent American feminists to speak out and work for much needed social, health, and educational improvements for women in those parts of the world engaged in the terrorist war with the United States illustrates how strongly such feminists, in a cutting-off-your-nose-to spite-your-face exercise, reject their homeland.[41]

The men and women of America's newest left are devout ideologues, convinced of their Truth and convinced that, if obstacles (i.e. the Western tradition) to that Truth are removed at home and abroad, all will see that Truth and be set free. As stated before, the very core of this Truth is an oxymoron, a deeply held pragmatic belief that all values are relative. Paradoxically they are highly moralistic. The Truth will prevail over the weaknesses and failings of American culture.

Though they would mightily and bitterly resist the assertion, their secular ideology constitutes a religion, if religion is thought of as any system of thoughts or beliefs that defines ultimate reality and the meaning of life. As early as the 1960s, Richard Hofstadter, Pulitzer-prize-winning historian and critic of American political/religious Traditionalists (he identified early twentieth century Progressive reform as yet another manifestation of Protestant revivalism) early on saw, and warned against, the American Left moving rapidly to transform its politics into a religion. The Left resists such assertions and observations because to accept themselves as believers would make them too much like so many they oppose and would turn their own arguments or confessions—such as the Truth of Science—back on themselves.[42]

They are Secularists for the very reason that, in order to pursue their own perceived virtues and their own freedom, they have had to oppose and reject what they understand religion to be for most people, especially the foundational faith of the American nation. It is for the Ideologue yet another irony, an intentionally unrecognized one, for it was the development of religious bodies and the growth of religious faith in the United States that created and insisted on a pluralistic, secular society, precisely so that all could have that most elemental of freedoms, freedom of belief.[43]

Religion as practiced by most in the United States eventually points to God, tradition, or collective wisdom that suggests absolutes, even if seen dimly or barely understood. The holy writ of America as a secular nation cannot be understood and has no meaning outside the concept of God creating man to be free. It runs through Jefferson's Declaration of Independence, Lincoln's Gettysburg Address and Second Inaugural ("with firmness in the right, as God gives us to see the right") and Martin Luther King, Jr.'s "I Have a Dream," with both Lincoln and King pointing back to Jefferson's words justifying the creation of a new nation "under God": "that all men are created equal; that they are endowed by their Creator with certain unalienable rights; that among these are life, liberty. . . ." God, man, freedom, and eventually nation have been tied together from the days of the Pilgrims' City on a Hill and the founding of Roger Williams' and William Penn's Holy Experiment, new Israel colonies and the Great Awakening of the 1740's presaging the Revolution for Independence. But Professor George Lakoff of the University of California at Berkley adds a different slant to the image of American, religious Traditionalists. Christian Traditionalists are those Americans wanting freedom for no one but themselves (white males) and wanting women at home and all minorities held in a second-class status. If so, these Traditionalists must be extraordinarily inept and dim-witted, or at least never a majority setting traditionalist standards, for they have certainly taken a multitude of political actions (including Constitutional amendments) in direct opposition to their desires.[44]

This American myth runs throughout the history of American foreign relations from the first days of the nation's full emergence onto the world's stage, from the 1898 Spanish-American War on to the present, from America's moment of destiny under Wilson to make the world safe for democracy to Truman's promise that the United States would protect the freedom of its allies, to Kennedy's "the rights of man come not from the generosity of the state, but from the hand of God . . . let the word go forth . . . *that we will pay any price* [emphasis added] . . . to assure the survival and the success of liberty," to President George W. Bush's reiteration that freedom is the God-given right of all people. To his fellow citizens of Massachusetts Irish Catholic Kennedy in the week before his inauguration spoke of the vision he shared with the state's Puritan forefathers: the United States was today's "city upon a hill."[45]

Today's Secular Ideologues, like so many before them, see only the blindness of other's faiths and the evils wrought in the name of religion. They refuse to see religion in the United States as the wellspring of freedom and the impulse behind many of the advances in human well-being there and elsewhere. They hold up President Bush's words that repeat these very sentiments, that tie nation (and world), God, and freedom together, as proof of his unhealthy ties to a dangerous reactionary Christianity.

Though not as Lakoff defines the situation, the old religion does assert values concerning gender and gender preference that can and do sharply clash with the values of the Secularists. And Secularists remember the devout who defended slavery and segregation (they ignore the devout behind almost all political/social reforms in the United States) and what they (the Ideologues) label patriarchy, all as the will of God. They see outside the United States theocracies and the intolerant devout and too much fear the same in America while incredibly ignoring the far greater threat elsewhere.

Further the Secularists wish to banish religion, at least from all public life, because it confronts them too personally. Two 2008 movies illustrate this. In *Religulous* atheist Bill Maher debunks all religion, asserting its harmful effect. Ben Stein in *Expelled: No Intelligence Allowed* lays out academia's censorship of thought and exclusion of religious intellectuals (an oxymoron to Secularist), illustrating how wide-spread and deep such censorship is. Religion, as preached in the United States, means not only freedom, but also personal restraint and absolutes and warnings against pride (as in Lincoln's referring to the Americans as perhaps the half-chosen people). Religion frames political debates within questions of ought and should, not pragmatism and the "The Truth of Science"—Senator John Kerry's use of this phrase suggests he never spent much time contemplating Faust or reading Mary Shelley's *Frankenstein*. Religion reminds them of Renan's warning to his fellow free-thinker Taine:

> You and I are living on a shadow. You're a decent man, and I'm a decent man, if you will, because we are operating on the Christian ethical code which was given us, infused with the Christian faith. Though we have lost the faith, we re-tain its shadow—which is the ethics. But what will happen to our children? We are living on the shadow of the lost faith, but we are not transmitting the faith to our children, along with the ethics. We are not giving them an ethics warmed up with a religious faith. They are living on the shadow of a shadow.

The old religion asserts that evil is not only societal but personal and that a decent man is still prone to sin, to miss the mark, to lose his lonely way.[46]

This belief is entirely too much restriction on the Secular Ideologues personal and public life. Ultimately the American Secularist is a visionary who righteously attacks evil while confidently rejecting the Western concept of tragedy—perhaps the subliminal reason many American universities no longer require English majors to study Shakespeare, yet another terrible irony, for he was in so many ways a radical. For the Secularists the great myths of American history and religion only obscure and cultivate evil repression. Therefore, the old histories of Western civilization that includes triumphs as well as defeats must not be taught and religious thought and motivation must be removed from public life. Actually the Secular Ideologues have trouble with the very idea of studying history. Having cut off themselves, as well as others, from history and religion, the Secular Ideologues cannot see that that act, their existential blow for freedom, has actually denied it to those who do not think as they, the very people they at least told themselves they were helping to be free alongside themselves.

THE POLITICAL POWER OF THE SECULAR IDEOLOGUES

The Secular Ideologues have alliances at home and abroad that encourage them to think a new day is coming. Their own aspirations and the encouragement they receive also help them avoid introspection.

They have much in common today with many Western Europeans who, themselves, have stronger traditions of communist visions and/or existentialist thought. In much of Europe freedom and pure secularism have been identical. Much of Europe does not have a deep tradition of religious pluralism sustaining a desire and drive for liberty and undergirding a secular government. Rather, for many it was the ancient regime and its Church or nothing.

Any aberrant religious groups, for those who grew up in a state church culture, really were not viewed as possible new faith homes or anything upon which freedom could be established. The choice was the one, old religious faith once associated with repressive government and social structures or no faith.

American campuses in their drives for politically correct speech have taken on the values of both old religious Europe and modern, secular Europe while rejecting the far greater freedom found in the First Amendment that made and continues to make the United States the truly radically free state. In Europe secular governments bow to religious heritage by enforcing laws against libeling other's faiths or saying disagreeable things. So, the government sentences a man to jail for stating there was no holocaust and an Italian journalist, Oriana Fallaci, at the time of her death was on trial at the behest of Moslem leaders for defaming Islam (she had denounced Europe's toleration for what she called an Islamic invasion). Both Pope Benedict XVI and Muslim leaders have called for the governments of Europe to prohibit people from disparaging someone else's religion. In the United States, on the other hand, religious freedom is the first freedom and that freedom allows anyone to speak his/her mind free of any public or private censors who might claim offense to someone else's faith. Quite obviously if the government can be brought in to protect religious sensitivities, then someone or anyone can claim that eating chocolate bunnies on Easter is sacrilege and must be stopped. In England people, bowing to insistent Muslims, no longer advertise anything having any relation to hogs. There is no end to such oppression and suppression.[47]

Beyond strictly religious freedom concerns, American campuses now take the European political party approach when it comes to intellectual diversity. As Thomas Sowell has pointed out, it is not allowed. It is not allowed because the Truth is already known, so why tolerate anything else; more insidious is the attitude that no one with any real intellectual aptitude could think differently. On one university campus a well-honored senior professor led her students in tearing down the public protest crosses anti-abortion students had set up, claiming her action was an expression of free speech. Apparently the offending students' free speech rights did not matter. Universities assess the dispositions of students who would be teachers according to politically correct standards comparable to those of the Secular Ideologues, such as opposition to "institutional racism, classicism, and heterosexism," in whatever manner those "isms" are defined by those in the know. Universities and their students deny people like Ward Connerly a forum to argue the merits or lack of same of affirmative action, while at the University of Kentucky (hardly an elitist Ivy League school), its Women and Gender Studies Program, chaired by a lesbian philosophy professor, uses public funds to fly in a fellow philosophy professor from Oregon to lecture on why men need to be banished from all political participation (voting and holding office) in the United States, until they have been resocialized. All this conforms to Brandeis Professor Herbert Marcuse's 1965 essay "Repressive Tolerance" in which Marcuse urged academics to repress conservatives and their speech because in doing so they were legitimately resisting the "repressive status quo."[48]

Also, in Europe war has not been a somewhere else occurrence. Its atrocities have been well-known and on home soil and nearly constant until the peace afforded Western Europe by the Cold War standoff between communism/ totalitarianism and capitalism/republicanism. Exhausted by conflict, aghast at their self-inflicted horrors, and then relatively free of standing in the breech between East and West, Europe had an exhausted, desperate hope for a world of no more war and experienced a long time (comparatively speaking) of peace. They rested and some, it seems, began to think that that rest was a natural condition. In February, 2009, the President of France found himself asking delegates to the Munich European Security Conference "Does Europe want peace [and the price it entails] or do we want to be left alone in peace?" In 2002, the Finnish prime minister in a London speech stated: "the EU [European Union] must not develop into a military superpower but must become a great power that will not take up arms at any occasion in order to defend its own interests."[49]

Furthermore, once the Eastern threat declined, Western Europe had a natural and reasonable fear of a hegemony from the still farther West, the United States. Nations' self-expression, autonomy, and unrestricted development free of entanglement with the United States parallels the hopes of American Secularists for internal social/political developments within their own nation. For American Secularists, the coalescence of nations inside the European Union and the use of the World Court and a concomitant European legal insistence on politically correct thought and speech regarding feminism, gay rights, and religion in public life can be seen as yet another parallel to their efforts to build a new order at home of race/ethnic/gender coalitions in opposition to an overbearing WASP nation with its myths of exceptionalism.

Domestically, America's Secularists have, by association, considerable political power, and by position, considerable opportunity to preach and pronounce. As already noted, Secularists hold great prominence in academia, which has become almost a world unto itself claiming the privileges of tenure from a public it typically disdains. David Horowitz in his *The Professors: the 101 Most Dangerous Professors in America* has identified adamantly antitraditionalist academics in public institutions many of whom have served as presidents of their particular national professional associations. In the latter part of the twentieth century, America's leading universities no longer require courses in American history for graduation, but they have increased the number of ethnic and gender history courses, making them major school programs.[50]

Much of the Secularists' political power comes from being members of (and organizing within) the longest continuously existing political party in the world, the American Democratic Party, which for much of its existence has been (and remains today) a massing of disparate group interests not necessarily of one accord on all things except their common opposition to the nation's cultural and power center which from the Civil War on has been represented more by the Republican Party and its identity with dissenting English Protestantism (hence the often-used acronym WASPs).

Historically this massing of separate interests has been a cause and effect of the Democratic Party's serving as a conduit for those on the periphery moving closer to the middle. The Democratic Party, at least until the rise of the Secularists, has been the means for the gradual amalgamation of such people into traditional culture. But that amalgamation also over time has meant a gradual shifting of identity by many to the Republican Party. Keeping people non-English speaking severely retards the amalgamation and keeps such people more loyal to the Party that provides the Secularists a means for changing the cultural landscape of the nation.

In truth, despite its history since the New Deal, the Democratic Party no longer is the party of a pragmatism bridging sometimes-clashing subcultures. It is the party of pragmatism only until it wins the government. Campaigning, it denounces the Republican infusion of values issues as divisive and often as an unconstitutional intrusion of religion into secular affairs. But once in office the rules of the game change. Then, "it's about racial quotas, mainstreaming gay culture, scrubbing the public Square of Christianity, and a host of explicitly cultural ambitions."[51]

This can be seen in the 2008 Presidential election and the newly elected Democratic President's first actions. Candidate Obama, choosing his place and time (San Francisco) made light of Traditionalists, saying they relied on religion and guns. Generally, though, he presented himself as above all else a man who could empathize with all, even the religious, or most especially the religious, and who would as President be a problem solver. Then in his inaugural address he paraphrased St Paul, telling those not his allies (it would seem) that it was time to put away childish things. He bowed to the Left immediately on two issues of no practicality that restricted the liberty of conservatives, rescinding Bush's order that public funds not be sent abroad in support of abortion counseling and rescinding Bush's regulation that health care institutions document that they respected the religious right of employees not to participate in abortions or reproductive services. In neither instance did he have to act. In the first instance he made certain taxpayers would aid abortion services against their will, and in the second he made uncertain the job security of not-sound thinking people. Taking no action would not have denied any of the rights claimed by Secularists. Taking action, however, meant using the power of the central government to force a uniformity within society and a compliance with the central tenets of liberal ideology.[52]

This level of deception and the bending of the normal meaning of words to the breaking point are seen even more clearly in President Obama's renewal of federal spending for stem cell research. The new President said his predecessor had inserted politics and religion where it did not belong and that all he was doing was freeing science to go where it will, to discover the facts, to see what can be done. The President instructed his Office of Science and Technology Policy to ensure that "the administration's decisions about public policy be guided by the most accurate and objective scientific advice available." This is self deception on a national scale. The fact that science can or may manipulate stem cells was never disputed, only whether it should. That is preeminently a question of morality and a question that must be answered by a people, a community, one way or another. The President and his Secularists had made a moral decision; they just did not want to face up to the responsibility or tell the public it could not escape its own responsibility to make moral choices. This is slinking toward the nihilism Niebuhr warned about. Pragmatism here denies the necessity of any values for a society. A nation cannot long hold together denying even the existence of values beyond those internal to each individual.[53]

As the above illustration suggests, the power of the Secularists through the Democratic Party has been, and is, substantial. Twenty-five percent of American voters attend religious services once a year or less. They are the Democratic counterweight to the Republican evangelicals. The ratio on academic campuses of Democrats to Republicans is 5:1; a generation ago there was near parity. National academic professional organizations strongly advocate Secularist positions. The National Educational Association, a bulwark of the Democratic Party, unrestricted by state or federal laws limiting public employees active participation in partisan campaigns, has advocated and gotten the creation of site-based councils dominated by school employees to make all personnel and curriculum decisions in public primary and secondary schools. The citizen-voter-taxpayer is assigned a minority vote on such councils. Usually such public school employees are one of the largest voting blocks in legislative and Congressional districts.[54]

The NEA is just one part of pink collar labor. Other governmental employees at all levels of government are a good part of organized women's labor, another pillar of the Democratic Party, like the employees of the nation's public universities, so much so that the Party is not just the party of government, but today is the government's party. This brings the Democratic Party and the United States closer to the culture of Europe with its greater socialism, powerful governmental unions, and governmental expenditures a larger portion of gross national product. This explains William Voegli's report in the *Wall Street Journal* that "A film producer, interviewed on the Upper West Side by the *New York Times* the day after the 2004 election, subscribed to this view: 'New York is an island off the coast of Europe,' she said, explaining how John Kerry could lose a national election while winning 83% of the votes in Manhattan." The Ivory Tower looks out over a far greater expanse of territory than just the university campuses and what its inhabitants see farther afield is appalling. Voegle quotes novelist Jane Smiley to good effect on this point, out there is "the unteachable ignorance of the red states."[55]

Strengthening the Party and magnifying Bill Bishop's *Big Sort*, is the nation's entertainment industry, most especially cinema. Roger L. Smith, author of *Blacklisting Myself: Memoir of a Hollywood Apostate in the Age of Terror*, writes that he was very much a part of a world that brooked no challenge and expected none to a far left of center group mind-set—daily, off-the-cuff Bush bashing was a way of identifying one's self to others as a member of polite society—until he, Smith, broke from the crowd.[56]

Also, the Democratic Party draws to it those numerous Americans who, since the 1960s, have rejected traditional family structures in favor of lifestyles more like those of Western Europe. Bishop, referencing the findings of Belgian demographer Ron Lesthaeghe, reports that white women in northern blue states were marrying less, divorcing and not remarrying, having children later and fewer of them. "It struck Lesthaeghe," says Bishop, "that the states that were the most like Western Europe in terms of family formation were also the most Democratic in recent U.S. presidential elections."[57]

The Secularists also have benefited from the fact that amalgamation is a process over generations and never quite a disappearing act. In the 1990s a Catholic priest, when asked to explain why his co-religionists were not more supportive of Republican candidates, given the church's strong support for many of the social/moral stances of the Republican Party, responded by saying the Republicans were just too Protestant. In the 2006 Congressional elections, Catholics proved to be the true swing voters as Democrats (with two Independents) won a two seat majority in the Senate and defeated thirty Republicans in the House, aided by the number of Republican-Catholic Senators declining by two (from 11 to 9) and the number of Democratic-Catholic Senators increasing by three (13 to 16) plus a drop of 15 in the number of Republican-Catholic Representatives (57 to 42) accompanied by an increase of 16 in Democratic-Catholic Representatives (72 to 88). In 2008 the nation's archbishops through the Catholic Campaign for Human Development had budgeted $1.3 million in grants to anti-capitalist ACORN that had been receiving federal money for supplying subprime mortgagees to banks but rescinded the authorization for the money after learning of ACORN's problems with a million dollar embezzlement of its funds. The number of Catholics in Congress went up slightly more in 2008. Not surprisingly the defeated Republicans attempted to regroup by electing as the new Chairman of the Republican National Committee a Roman Catholic African American from Maryland, once a border-state now the southern end of the northeast seaboard.[58]

This religious/cultural divide further helps the Secularists by giving them allies and fellow believers drawn from the ranks of men and women raised up in their own non-WASP cultures who have given up the devout faith and ways of their fathers and mothers on the way toward mainstream inculcation, but who have had no background experience and understanding or real intellectual or emotional association that would permit them to see or desire an identity with the old guard WASPS. For these people, much like their counterparts in Europe, there is no viable alternative religious faith and the drive for adult independence that takes them away from the old family ways also takes them into a more purely secular world.

There they are joined by a goodly number of transformed WASPs. Compounding the problem of preserving a common, traditionalist community and set of values is the long-term, almost inevitable, increasing secularization of American Protestantism that has always been intertwined with Enlightenment and rationalist values. Old mainline Protestants in the late twentieth century swung out of their ancestral Republican home into the Democratic Party (in part due to the Civil Rights movement), to be replaced (again in part due to the Civil Rights movement) with a resurgent evangelical element. As noted by George Marsden, American academia—in large part a creation of Protestants seeking Christ and freedom—took freedom to the edges of the universe and ran into themselves coming back with an ever-expanding notion of freedom and tolerance that no longer had room for Christ:

> Eventually . . . the logic of the nonsectarian ideals [such as democracy, justice, inclusion] which the Protestant establishment had successfully promoted in public life dictated that liberal Protestantism itself should be moved to the periphery to which other religious perspectives had been relegated for some time. The result was an "inclusive" higher education that resolved the problems of pluralism by virtually excluding all religious perspectives from the nation's highest academic life . . . in other words, [today] the free exercise of religion does not extend to the dominant intellectual centers of our culture.[59]

This certainly is not true of all. As many historians have noted, the United States is a land of highly democratized Christianity and "Baptistification"— and in some ways it is, because of its Protestant pluralism, the Western world's most religious (high percentage of believers) and most secular of nations (First Amendment). Most find the not-necessarily-logical-in-terms-of-ideology melding of secularism and religion very appealing as a definition of freedom. Here nuns tell the touring Pope they want to be heard and parishioners try to buy church property away from their Bishop. As Huntington has written, in the United States the universal Church is really the American Catholic Church.[60]

Nevertheless, Southern Baptist Bill Clinton was not only the first "black" President but also a reincarnation of FDR; and the Democratic Party does hold together so long as it avoids cultural value issues while campaigning and concentrates on class/money issues. Clinton, himself, once in office had to be reminded of this when he hoped to have gays openly in the military. And within the Democratic Party, wins for the Party can be a measure of hope for Secular Ideologues that their cause can go on, even when, perhaps especially when, their cause is not an election issue. When they help the Party win they can expect rewards, especially and most immediately in terms of funding university teaching, research, and other programs, and the strengthening of bureaucracy, and, more, long-term, the liberalization of the federal courts.

To reiterate a grim, deep, multilayered irony of all this is that the Secular Ideologues, in pursuing individual freedom by consolidating Party power through a powerful, ever-more intrusive government, have measurably reduced liberty in the United States. Campuses are like Europe and Canada in the realm of free speech. There is none, only what is politically correct. Secondary and primary public schools are run by the employees. The federal bureaucracy and the federal courts at times have discarded congressional law and insisted that affirmative action means discriminating on the basis of race/gender/ethnicity in order to be nondiscriminatory, that equality is equality of outcome structured by the government, not equality of opportunity. African-American Mary Frances Berry, Geraldine R. Segal professor of social thought and professor of history at the University of Pennsylvania, Assistant Secretary for Education under Jimmy Carter and long-time Democratic member and Chair of the United States Civil Rights Commission has even stated that "Civil Rights law were not passed to give civil rights protection to all Americans." Feminists continue to demand that the government, not the market, compare and contrast employees' credentials (education and training) and rule on what is comparable from one field of knowledge to another and one job/profession to another (presumably all Ph.D.s would make whatever surgeons make) and in this manner define and require equal pay for equal work. Any semblance of a free market would no longer exist. Labor unions continue to insist on open ballots when voting on union representation. Through the Community Reinvestment Act passed under Jimmy Carter and President Clinton's executive orders implementing the law the federal government required loan institutions to offer subprime loans to people based on gender and race, making irrelevant monetary/credit qualifications for the loans, the underlying cause of the 2008–2009 national economic meltdown. In September 2008 Terry Jones in *Investor's Business Daily* wrote that President Clinton "turned the two quasi-private mortgage-funding firms [Fannie Mae and Freddie Mac] into a semi-nationalized monopoly that dispensed cash to markets, made loans to large Democratic voting blocs and handed favors, jobs, and money to political allies. This potent mix led inevitably to corruption and Fannie-Freddie collapse." Men may have a sense of lost economic liberty, since eighty percent of the jobs lost in the melt down were held by men while President Obama's recovery plan, despite the touted construction/infrastructure funds, is estimated to create far more jobs for women (especially in government) than they lost and not nearly as many jobs for men as they lost, so much so women are expected for the first time in the nation's history to surpass men in the number employed. Rubbing salt in the wounds, with men for a generation performing far behind women in schools and with women, according to a 2007 U. S. Department of Labor sponsored study, being fifty-one percent of all workers in high paying management, professional and related occupations, President Obama bowed to his Secular supporters by creating the White House Council on Women and Girls "to ensure that all Cabinet-level agencies consider how their policies affect women and families." There is, of course, no comparable office for men and families.[61]

QUO VADIS

No one can say with certainty what the future holds for America's Secular Ideologues. They may create their new world as their party, their vehicle for power, achieves a measure of success. More and more Americans say they have no religious faith, especially those living in the Pacific Northwest and in New England. In 2007 "births to unwed mothers reached an all-time high of about 40 percent" continuing a long-time upward trend. Many such unwed mothers have made a conscious decision to have children without husbands. Or over time their party may dull their ideological zealousness, or if the signal events and issues that made them—war (Vietnam and then Iraq), the civil rights era, and birth control/abortion—fade into that, as they see it, black hole of history, they too may fade. Most likely there will be a measure of ebb and flow for them and their romantic rejection of capitalist structures and exploitation and their rationalist trust in man's ability to recreate or redefine himself.[62]

Most likely, also, some version of the old order will remain. Most Americans are religious pragmatists or, another way of saying it, secular religious, the very definition of American traditionalism. Again, they are the quintessential collective individualists, finding ways to work together to produce group effort and create community while guarding individual liberty. Many find religious organizations providing the best way for families to express all this, even if such people also can be found under any one or more labels of group rights and prerogatives used by the Secularists, who have never realized that the rich tapestry of diversity they dream of and seek to design and create already exists, all the richer for having no master weavers forcing the design, with people free to live in many worlds of identity at once. Traditional religion in the United States will continue to preach about the inevitable intertwining of human nature and tragedy. Sexual relations will for the blessed remain a sacred mystery dance far above the Ideologue's parceling of freedoms and roles. Capitalism, within a democratic body politic, will still provide a way for more to have more.

Sometimes the new order's prophets cannot see the obvious. The First Amendment of the United States Constitution that came out of the American Revolution recognizes absolute rights/freedoms, though through a glass darkly, and protects the fundamental freedoms of speech, association and religion. Many of the founders of the United States, such as Washington, Adams, Jefferson, and Paine, were so-called free thinkers themselves, rejecting competing denominational dogmas. Sounding much like today's Secularists, Jefferson said of himself: "I am of a sect by myself as far as I know; and Paine: "My own mind is my own church." But the Secular Ideologues refuse to track the freethinking part of their DNA back to the American Revolution because almost all the founders believed religion and the absolutes and ethics it provided were necessary to the preservation of republican institutions. Not coincidentally were many of the founders Freemasons asserting the Fatherhood of God, the brotherhood of all men, and liberty of conscience as a right given to them by God. Nor do the Secular Ideologues wish to contemplate that much of the rest of the world saw the new country as a *Dangerous Nation* (the title of Robert Kagan's book) precisely because of its exaltation of both structured, republican, majoritarian authority and freedom. Lincoln in the middle of his country's Civil War calls the United States "the last best hope of earth" because at the time Great Britain was the only nation of any size with a stable elected government, and even there only a tiny fraction of the populace was entitled to vote. All this the Secularists seek to hide by not teaching American history and/or labeling the United States' particular manifestation of Western civilization as so corrupt as to be irredeemable. As existentialists they are not about historical perspective.[63]

The Ideologues, however, do track their DNA back to the French Revolution and its glorification and deification of the Natural Man and the Goddess Reason, never acknowledging that none of the would-be Natural Men in their great drive for equality could ever figure out or agree upon exactly what the goddess was saying, and thus freedom devolved into murderous madness and authoritarianism. The Secular Ideologues refuse to see that in such a world everyone tends to fall back to the first of the medieval seven deadly sins, Pride, and become gods unto themselves, modern men and women, as Jung has said, running around searching for their souls. Think Jean Paul Sartre.

As children of light, the Secular Ideologues sometimes can be the "salt of the earth," providing a necessary corrective to complacency, privilege (as opposed to rights), and injustice. But the rage of these Americans, free to criticize and free to restructure, is sometimes more about man's ages old personal desire to be free from the weight of history and the constraints of human nature. Sometimes it is paradoxically about their own unrecognized, not confessed, primordial longing for more personal blood/ethnic ties—mankind's apparently-never-disappearing tribalism now at times naïve and even masquerading as universalism—and very often about subconsciously enshrining (perhaps because of another deep primordial need) their politics as the new, more inspired religious creed, not really so much about perceived societal/political ills. Accordingly the rage directed at their national home is not always justified even by the terms of equality and justice they have set out.

Notes

FREEDOM IN RELIGION

1. For thoughts on the importance of dissenting English Protestantism in the creation of an American culture see Ernest Tuveson, *Redeemer Nation: The Idea of America's Millennial Role* (Chicago, 1968) and Samuel Huntington, *Who Are We? The Challenges to America's National Identity* (New York: Simon & Schuster, 2004).

2. Richard Hofstadter, *The Age of Reform: From Bryan to F.D.R.* (New York: Alfred A. Knopf, 1956), 8–9.

3. Eldon Eisenach, *The Lost Promise of Progressivism* (Lawrence, Kansas: University Press of Kansas, 1994), 4, 7.

4. David Chidester, *Patterns of Power: Religion and Politics in American Culture* (Englewood Cliffs, 1988); Nathan Hatch, *The Democratization of American Christianity* (New Haven, 1989); Jonah Goldberg, *Liberal Fascism, The Secret History of The American Left from Mussolini to the Politics of Meaning* (New York: Doubleday, 2007), 213.

5. Allan J. Lichtman, *White Protestant Nation: The Rise of the American Conservative Movement* (New York: Atlantic Monthly Press, 2008), 4.

6. David Crary, "Students steal, cheat, see themselves as quite ethical," Lexington *Herald-Leader*, December 1, 2008, A3.

7. Dinesh D'Souza, *The Enemy at Home: The Cultural Left and Its Responsibility for 9/11* (New York: Doubleday, 2007), 66: Pew Forum, "How Church Attendance Affects Religious Voting Patterns," *http://pewforum .org/docs/?DecID=364,November24.2008*; Lydia Saad, "Blacks Postgrads Young Adults Help Obama Prevail, *http://www.gallup.com/poll/111781/ Blacks-Postgrads-YoungAdults-Help-Obama-Prevail.aspxNov6,2008*;

Nicholas Kristof, "Conservative givers beat liberal tightwads," Lexington *Herald-Leader*, December 23, 2008, A11.

8. Richard Carwardine, *Evangelicals and Politics in Antebellum America* (New Haven: Yale University Press, 1993), 2–3; Hofstadter, 24–46, 127, 152; Fr. John S Rausch, "Declaration of Human Rights remains a vision rather than an accomplishment," *Crossroads*, January 18, 2009, 14; Martha C. Nussbaum, *Liberty of Conscience: In Defense of America's Tradition of Religious Equality* (New York: Basic Books, 2008), 8–9, 82–83.

9. Thomas Cahill writes how "The Jews gave us . . . our outlook and our inner life. . . . We dream Jewish dreams and hope Jewish hopes. Most of our best words, in fact—new, adventure, surprise; unique, individual, person, vocation; time, history, future; freedom, progress, spirit; faith, hope, justice—are the gifts of the Jews." Thomas Cahill, *The Gifts of the Jews: How a Tribe of Desert Nomads Changed the Way Everyone Thinks and Feels* (New York: Nan A. Tales/Anchor Books, 1998), 240–241; it was a Jewish rabbi and a Jewish Pharisee who added the word "love": Dinesh D'Souza, "Created Equal: How Christianity Shaped the West," *Imprints*, Vol. 37, No. 11, 1–5.

10. For a discussion of this exceptionalism/universalism see Dinesh D'Souza, *What's so Great About America* (New York: Penguin Books, 2003), 161.

11. Ecclesiastes 3:11. Concerning the Christian concept of joy see Frederick Buechner, *Listening to Your Life* (San Francisco: HarperSanFrancisco, 1992), 272–3, 286–288, and C.S. Lewis, *Surprised by Joy* (London: Harvest Books, 1955).

12. Genesis 4: 1–15; Michael Kammen, *People of Paradox: An Inquiry Concerning the Origins of American Civilization* (New York: Vintage Boos, 1973).

13. For an analysis of social isolation as a product of diversity see Russell K. Nieli, "Diversity's Discontents: The Contact Hypothesis Exploded," *Academic Questions*, Vol.21, No. 4, 409–430, and Robert Putnam, *Bowling Alone: The Collapse and Revival of American Community* (New York: Simon and Schuster, 2000) and Gregory Rodriguez, "Diversity breeding distrust isolation," Lexington *Herald-Leader*, August 19, 2007, C1–C2.

14. For an examination of expansion and integration of new communities with older ones see Paul Conkin, *Cane Ridge: America's Pentecost* (Madison: University of Wisconsin Press, 1990) and Christopher Waldrep, "The Making of a Border State Society: James McCready, the Great Revival, and the Prosecution of Profanity in Kentucky," *The American Historical Review*, Vol. 99, No. 3, 767–784.

15. David Riesman, *The Lonely Crowd* (New Haven: Yale University Press, 1950); Natan Sharansky, *Defending Identity: Its Indispensable Role*

in Protecting Democracy (New York: Public Affairs, 2008); Rod Dreher, "Loving Our Limits: the Times Catch Up to Kentucky's Wendell Berry," Lexington *Herald-Leader*, November 27, 2008, A21.

16. Proverbs 29:18; I Corinthians 13.

17. George Weigel, *The Cube and the Cathedral: Europe, America and Politics Without God* (New York: Basic Books, 2005), 166.

18. Helen Keller's *Let Us Have Faith* as quoted by *http://www.nsrider.com/quotes/life.htm12/3/08.*

19. For a study of the clash of liberty and democracy in America and the dangers of mass democracy see Fareed Zakaria, *The Future of Freedom: Illiberal Democracy at Home and Abroad* (W. W. Norton & Company, 2007).

20. Goldberg notes the possibility always of populist movement on the right, *Liberal Fascism*, 396.

21. For a discussion of free speech in the United States and less free speech in much of the rest of the West see Adam Lipstak, "Unlike Others, U.S. Defends Freedom to Offend in Speech," *http://www.nytimes.com/2008/06/12/us/12hate.html?pogwanted-l&_r=1&partner=rssnyt...*

22. Galatians 3:28.

23. Kathleen Parker, "Preacher responded to real concerns of churchgoers in uncertain decadent times," Lexington *Herald-Leader* May 20, 2008, D2; Parker, "Fewer dads no cause to celebrate," Lexington *Herald-Leader*, March 26, 2006; D'Souza, *Enemy*, 66; Janet Kornblum, "More women 40 to 44 remaining childless," *USA Today*, August 19, 2008, 12B: *Pew Forum*; Kristof; Rodriquez.

24. Gallup Poll, October 27–November 2 on presidential candidate preference.

25. Jonah Goldberg, "Just how crazy are the Dems," *Los Angeles Times*, May 15, 2007, A15; Kornblum; David Lightman and Margaret Talev, "Obama sees hope in faces: Half-million fill National Mall, stars perform before inauguration," Lexington *Herald-Leader*, January 19, 2009, A5.

26. African American David Ehrenstein in March of 2007 in the *Los Angeles Times* referred to Obama as the Magic Negro, saying he really was a black man that white people wanted, a benign black man with cross-cultural appeal, one that would allow white people to assuage their guilt, but not really a man of black culture. Larry Elder, "Obama the Magic Negro-Gate," *http://TownHall.com/columnists/LarryElder/2009/01/01Obama_the_Magic_Negro_gate;* "Ayers Turned away from Canada by Immigration Officials," http://www.foxnews.com/politics/2009/01/19/Ayers-turned-away-canada-immigration-officials/

FREEDOM FROM RELIGION

1. Samuel Huntington, *Who Are We? The Challenges to America's National Identity* (New York: Simon & Schuster, 2004), 270.

2. Series finale of American Broadcasting Company's television series "Boston Legal," December 8, 2008.

3. Art Jester, "Tackling Domestic Partner Benefits," Lexington *Herald-Leader,* 1 Jan. 2007.

4. Huntington, 40, 64, 68, 83–84.

5. Michael Kammen, *People of Paradox: an Inquiry Concerning the Origins of American Civilization* (New York: Random House, 1972); Martin Marty, "Baptistification Takes Over," *Christianity Today,* 27(1983), 33–35.

6. Robert Kagan, *Dangerous Nation: America's Place in the World from Its Earliest Days to the Dawn of the Twentieth Century* (New York: Alfred A. Knopf, 2006)

7. Richard Hofstadter, *The Age of Reform: From Bryan to F.D.R.* (New York: Alfred A Knopf, 1956), 8–9; Jay Dolan, *The American Catholic Experience: a History From Colonial Times to the Present* (Garden City: University of Notre Dame Press, 1985), 244–245, 312–318.

8. Robert Wiebe, *Self-rule: a Cultural History of American Democracy*(Chicago: University of Chicago Press, 1995), 147, 184, 209–210.

9. Eldon J. Eisenach, *The Lost Promise of Progressivism* (Lawrence: University Press of Kansas, 1994).

10. Reinhold Niebuhr, *The Children of Light and the Children of Darkness: A Vindication of Democracy and a Critique of Its Traditional Defense* (New York: Charles Scribner's Sons, 1944).

11. Niebuhr, 130–135.

12. Carol Innannone, "Family Matters: a Conversation with David Popenae," *Academic Questions,* XX, 1, 20–21.

13. Huntington, 48.

14. *Lexington Herald,* April 20, 2004; Martha C. Nussbaum, *Liberty of Conscience: In Defense of America's Tradition of Religious Equality* (New York: Basic Books, 2008), 4, 6, 9, 112; Thomas L. Krannawitter, *Vindicating Lincoln: Defending the Politics of Our Greatest President* (Lanham: Rowman & Littlefield, 2008), 250.

15. Dinesh D'Souza, *The Enemy at Home: The Cultural Left and Its Responsibility for 9/11* (New York: Doubleday, 2007), 265.

16. D'Souza, 141.

17. D'Souza, 67.

18. Bill Bishop, *The Big Sort: Why The Clustering of Like-Minded America is Tearing Us Apart* (Boston: Houghton Mifflin, 2008), 200–209, 214, 216.

19. David Blankenhorn, *Fatherless America: Confronting Our Most Urgent Social Problem* (New York: Basic Books, 1995), 67, 3, 90, 122.

20. Blankenhorn, 4, 54, 208–211,128–219, 30.

21. Bishop, 209–211; Lecture by Bill Bishop at Joseph-Beth Bookstore in Lexington, Kentucky, July 14, 2008.

22. Lani Guinier, *The Tyranny of the Majority* (New York: Free Press, 1994).

23. *United Steel Workers of America* v. *Weber* (443 U.S.193, 1979); Kentucky Cabinet for Families and Children, Affirmative Action Program, Nov. 1999.

24. *Roe* v. *Wade* (410 U.S. 113, 1973).

25. Blankenhorn, 67.

26. John Leo, "What Larry meant to say," *U.S. News & World Report*, 14 Feb. 2005; Matt Crenson, "A matter of gray and white matter; studies suggest sexes use brain differently," Lexington *Herald-Leader*, 28 Feb. 2005; Ellen Goodman, "Stay-at-home moms should know the risks," Lexington *Herald-Leader*, 6 Jan. 2006; George Weigel, "Europe's Two Culture Wars, What Happens when radical relativism meets mass Muslim immigration," *Commentary*, Vol.121, No. 5, May 2006, 29–36.

27. Allan Bloom, *The Closing of the American Mind: How Higher Education Has Failed Democracy and Impoverished the Souls of Today's Students* (New York: Simon &Schuster, 1987), 102, 114.

28. Bloom, 99.

29. Alan Brinkley, *American History, a Survey*, 12th ed., (Boston: McGraw-Hill, 2006), 517.

30. Christine Hoff Sommers, *The War Against Boys: How Misguided Feminism Is Harming our Young Men* (New York: Simon & Schuster, 2000), 102–122.

31. John Leo, "Stomping on Free Speech," *U.S. News & World Report*, April 19, 2004, 14.

32. Merlene Davis on children of gay couples, Lexington *Herald-Leader*, December 12, 2006, D1.

33. Norval D. Glenn, "Family Textbooks Twelve Years Later," *Academic Questions*, XXII, 1, 83; Daniel Cere, "Human Rights and the Family," *Academic Questions*, xxii, 77, 70.

34. Blankenhorn, 22.

35. Peter Wood, *Diversity: The Invention of a Concept* (San Francisco: Encounter Books, 2003); Ruben J. Nazario, "Assimilation robs U.S., immigrants," Lexington *Herald-Leader*, 3 Apr. 2006.

36. Jeffrey Hart, *Smiling Through the Cultural Catastrophe: Toward the Revival of Higher Education* (New Haven: Yale University Press, 2001), 246–247.

37. Huntington, 272–273.

38. Dan Carey, "America needs leaders who promote peace, not war," Lexington *Herald-Leader*, 4 Dec. 2006, A11.

39. Michael Fogler, "Violence doesn't make the world better," Lexington *Herald-Leader*, 21 Dec. 2006, A11.

40. For examples of the Secular Ideologues' mind set see George Lakoff, *Whose Freedom? The Battle over America's Most Important Idea* (New York: Farrar, Straus and Giroux, 2006).

41. Mark Steyn, "Prime Minister Obama," *National Review*, March 23, 2009, 22–24.

42. Hofstadter, 152; David S. Brown, *Richard Hofstadter: An Intellectual Biography* (Chicago: University of Chicago Press, 2006).

43. See Richard Neuhaus, ed., *Unsecular America* (Grand Rapids: Eedrman's, 1986).

44. As reported by Peter Berkowitz in his review of George Lakoff's *Whose Freedom? The Battle Over America's Most Important Idea* (New York: Farrar, Straus and Giroux, 2006) in *Policy Review* (Oct. and Nov. 2006), No. 139, 81–88.

45. *Policy Review*; James Piereson, "Lee Harvey Oswald & the Liberal Crack-up," *Commentary*, Vol. 121, No. 5, May 2006, 46.

46. *Religulous* (2008) and *Expelled: no Intelligence Allowed* (2008); Anecdote concerning Renan writing to Taine about 1860 as paraphrased by Will Durant in an article by Robert L. Payton in the *Courier-Journal-Louisville Times*, 12 Oct. 1975, D6.

47. Frances D'Emillo, "Italian journalist grilled world leaders," Lexington *Herald-Leader*, 16 Sept. 2006.

48. Thomas Sowell, "Faculty 'diversity' usually means left, and far left," Louisville *Courier-Journal*, 9 Jan. 2005; Brett Barrouquere, "Anti-abortion display dismantled," Lexington *Herald-Leader*, 24 Apr. 2006; John Leo, "Class(room) Warriors," *U.S. News & World Report*, 24 Oct. 2005; Jester, "Tackling Benefits"; Presentation by Dr. Naomi Zack at the University of Kentucky, 3–5 Nov. 2006; David Horowitz, *The Professors: The 101 Most Dangerous Academics in America* (Washington, D.C.: Regnery Publishing, Inc., 2006), xxxvi-xxxvii, 177–179, 223–226, 284–287, 152–155, 241–244, 167–170, 77–80, 227–229.

49. Mark Steyn, "Prime Minister Obama: will European statism supplant the American Way?" *National Review*, March 23, 2009, 22–24; Mark Steyn, "Happy Warrior: Helium Diplomacy," *National Review*, May 4, 2009, 56.

50. See Horowitz citation in end note #48.

51. Jonah Goldberg, *Liberal Fascism: The Secret History of the American Left from Mussolini to the Politics of Meaning* (New York: Doubleday, 2007), 359.

52. "Change? Now taxpayers will pay for abortions," *The Kentucky Citizen*, January/February, 2009, 6; Ricardo Alonso-Zaldivar, "Obama likely to rescind abortion rule," Lexington *Herald-Leader*, February 28, 2009, A4.

53. *Crossroads*, March 15, 2009, 1, 6.

54. D'Souza, 192; Horowitz, xxxv; The Kentucky Educational Reform Act of 1990.

55. William Voegeli, "The Roots of Liberal Condescension: Snobbery is the last refuge of the liberal arts major," *Wall Street Journal*, February 18, 2009; Bishop, 214–215.

56. Roger L. Simon, *Blacklisting Myself: Memoir of a Hollywood Apostate in the Age of Terror* (New York: Encounter Books, 2008).

57. Bishop, 214.

58. Lexington *Herald-Leader*, 26 Feb. 1995. Paula M. Kane, *Separation and Subculture: Boston Catholicism, 1900–1920* (Chapel Hill: 1994); Nancy Frazier O'Brien, "110th U.S. Congress the most religiously diverse ever," *Crossroads*, January 21, 2007; *Crossroads*, November 23, 2008, 4.

59. George M. Marsden, *The Soul of the American University: From Protestant Establishment to Established Nonbelief* (New York: Oxford University Press, 1994), 5–6.

60. Neuhaus; Huntington, 95.

61. Horowitz, 69; "Subprime" at *http://en.wikipedia.org/wiki/Community*; Kathleen Parker, "Even 'First Father' leaves boys out of family picture," Lexington *Herald Leader*, March 19, 2009, A11.

62. Rachel Zoll, "More in U.S. say they're not religious," Lexington *Herald Leader*, March 9, 2009, A4; Lance Dickie, "When it comes to religion, more are saying 'No Thanks,'" Lexington *Herald Leader*, March 26, 2009, A11; Mike Stobbe, "2007 U.S. births break record," Lexington *Herald Leader*, March 19, 2009, A4.

63. Edwin Gaustad and Leigh Schmidt, *The Religious History of America: the Heart of the American Story from Colonial Times to Today* (New York: HarperCollins, 2002), 132–138; Robert Kagan, *Dangerous Nation: America's Place in the World from It's Earliest Days to the Dawn of the Twentieth Century* (New York: Alfred A Knopf, 2006), 3–6; C. G. Jung, *Modern Man in Search of a Soul*, translated by W. S. Dell and Cary F. Baynes, paperback (New York: Harcourt Brace Janovich, n.d.), 196–220.

www.ingramcontent.com/pod-product-compliance
Lightning Source LLC
Chambersburg PA
CBHW021824270326
41932CB00007B/327